Advanced Prep for the New SAT Writing Section

VERY CHALLENGING PROBLEMS
FOR THOSE TARGETING PERFECT SCORES

Matthew Rudolph Larriva

Powerful Prep

Irvine, California

Matthew Larriva/Powerful Prep, Inc.
17595 Harvard Ave, Ste C #2320
Irvine CA, 92614
www.powerfulprep.com

Ordering Information:
Quantity sales. Special discounts are available on quantity purchases by corporations, associations, and others. For details, contact the address above.

Advanced Prep: SAT Writing
ISBN-13: 978-1519244505
ISBN-10: 1519244509

About this Book

This book has a single goal: moving students from near-perfection to perfection. For many, it's easy to move from the 60th percentile to the 90th, but nearly impossible to close the gap and move to that perfect score. If you don't have a good grasp over the fundamentals of grammar, then you might not be ready for this book, but if you're looking to boost your score and test your intellect though very challenging problems, then read on.

The reason many struggle to gain those last few points that separate Ivy-League scores from Tier 2 scores is simple: most test-prep material is too pedagogical. There is too much lecturing and too few problem sets. Exacerbating this problem is the fact that it is hard to find a large number of Level-5 (the most challenging) problems. When you're already scoring above 80% accuracy, you don't need instruction, and you don't need to waste time on Level 1 problems. What you need is Level 6 problems so that everything you come across on the test will seem easy to you. That's where Advanced Prep for the New SAT Writing Section comes in.

Working the problems on the following pages will make you a grammar genius, and will elevate your SAT score. The problems are very hard, the answer-explanations are thorough, and the chapters cover all skills necessary to move you to perfection.

How to Use This Book

Work linearly. Complete each chapter before moving on to the next. Then, after you are done with the grammar-specific chapters, move onto the Random Tests

This book is not written like an SAT test, but the questions are SAT-type questions. While the SAT is multiple choice and paragraph-style, this book, for the most part, is not.

In an effort to challenge you and develop your skills more fully, you are asked to fill in your own answers. By not having sample answers to process-of-eliminate or lean on, you will become stronger.

All the best,
Matt Larriva

Contents

Contents

This is for my sister: my partner in crime, my parents' greatest gift, and my perpetual confidant.

Let's eat grandma!
Let's eat, grandma!

PUNCTUATION IS IMPORTANT: GOOD GRAMMAR SAVES LIVES.

CHAPTER 1

Adjectives and Adverbs

You've heard that adjectives modify nouns and that adverbs modify verbs. It turns out this is a very elementary view of these parts of speech.

Adjectives can modify nouns and pronouns.

Adverbs can modify just about everything: verbs, adjectives, other adverbs, and strangely, nouns (if they are gerunds i.e. my running, his learning).

Pro Tip:

When you come to an adjective or an adverb, simply ask what it is referring to, or, what is it modifying? If it is modifying a noun or a pronoun, it should almost always be an adjective. If it is modifying a verb, adjective, adverb, or gerund, then it should almost always be an adverb. For the purposes of the SAT, nearly all adverbs will end in "ly."

Practice

Most of the following sentences contain an abused adjective or adverb. Circle the error if you find one.

1) I am doing good as the successful successor to the position of President of the Red Cross.

2) I am doing well as the successful successor to the position of President of the Red Cross.

3) The Frenchman is a sommelier and tastes quite good.

4) The Frenchman, who is a sommelier, was eaten by the cannibals who said he tasted quite well.

5) The Frenchman, who is a sommelier, was eaten by the cannibals who discussed his qualifications saying that he had a refined palate and tasted quite good.

6) The horse ran past the barn fell.

7) I have not studied late much late.

8) Lately as it was, I didn't mind being awoken by the clatter, for it meant that my wife had returned safely.

9) The mattress was hardly, so the orthopedists agreed it was far superior to the soft one in preventing lower back pain.

10) Because she is working so hardly she will most likely not have time for dining with us, which is unfortunate because I have prepared her favorite.

11) Because she is working hard she will most likely have time for dining with us, which is fortunate, because I have prepared her favorite.

12) If you stand up too fast you will develop lightheadedness and risk falling down.

13) To reach the oil will require not only extensive surveys by geologists but digging deeply by miners.

14) The reason we go downtown and to flea markets is in order to purchase things like scarves and rugs cheap.

15) She bakes miraculously well, and resultantly, her most recent creation tastes amazingly.

16) Though you may disagree with the adoption of the new core standards, you cannot refute that they were designed special for the district by the director of the Department of Education.

17) Pensive, the man considered his options and mulled their consequences.

18) Pensively, the man considered his options and mulled their consequences.

19) When you go fishing, if you catch an incredibly, rare tuna you would do well to put it back in the ocean.

20) When you go fishing, if you catch an incredible rare tuna you would do well to put it back in the ocean.

21) Maybe they are unique and manufactured by that infamous three-named designer, but these unbelievable expensive shoes simply cannot be worth either the price or the death of the alligator that was required for their construction.

22) I must insist that if you structure your sentence like that, then your pronoun is being used wrong.

23) The serene flowing river passes by the resort and provides the perfect environment for men to fish, for women to sunbathe, and for families to recreate.

24) It was said of the spy that he conducted himself ostentatious, and thus was the antithesis of what he needed to be.

25) Arguable the best film of the year was the cartoon, which is unlikely to win any grand jury prizes, but will reside in the hearts and minds of the audiences for quite some time.

26) In the space of the grand auditorium, and given the work that the benefactors had put into improving the acoustics so that the performances would resound better, the music sounds fully and good.

27) Funny enough, I was just mentioning to Sara last week that the way she walks is so staggeringly different from her sister's gait that it's hard to believe they're sisters.

28) Funny enough, the comedian would serve the purpose for which we hired him: to provide some background entertainment as the guests arrived.

29) I suppose that the moral of the story of the Tortoise and the Hare is that pacing oneself slow and steady wins the race.

30) It is arguable that the best film of the series will be the one produced most inexpensive, not the one which is an archetype of typical cinematic glut.

31) Cinematic showy movies are the stuff of awards shows and art house premiers, but I prefer a good cartoon any day.

32) Seeming errant methods of calculating the sum of non-converging series can be deceptively simple but also deceptively complex if executed incorrectly.

33) Obstreperous well-meaning boys are not the norm at our institution, as we are more the type of school that takes demure, knowledge-seeking gentlemen.

34) These errands are just eating away the daylight and my productivity, yet they are not necessary the most important things I will do today, despite the hours they require of me.

35) You cannot, nor should you try to fight the changing tide which so often overcomes us with its insidious encroaching rhythms which placate us one moment and drown us the next.

36) Insufficient funded classes are one of the main reasons that schools in certain countries are at such a disadvantage relative to others.

37) Seek not to operate in a way that brings you happiness, for that is the goal of children, but to conduct yourself in a method that is deliberate angling you toward long term peace and the betterment of those around you.

38) The pursuer is encouraged to send only one text message, to wait patient until his text message is responded to, and then to respond in kind after an appropriate amount of time has lapsed, as to not seem too eager.

39) The arbitrary arbiter, random and mercurial, errant, albeit not without noble motives, decided to side with the plaintiff in the pollution case.

40) A financial analyst, quantitatively-minded and good with computers, adroit, and with a strong fundamental knowledge of financial processes and valuations, is able to determine the value of equities and assign them relative ratings.

Answers

1) I am doing good as the successful successor to the position of President of the Red Cross.

   Correct as is. The person is doing good deeds.

2) I am doing well as the successful successor to the position of President of the Red Cross.

   Correct as is. The person is successful (he is performing well).

3) The Frenchman is a sommelier and tastes quite *well.*

   Left as is, it implies that if you ate the sommelier he would be tasty.

4) The Frenchman, who is a sommelier, was eaten by the cannibals who said he tasted quite *good.*

   The sentence implied that the sommelier was tasty to consume: he tasted good.

5) The Frenchman, who is a sommelier, was eaten by the cannibals who discussed his qualifications saying that he had a refined palate and tasted quite *well.*

   Here we are told that the cannibals were referring to his skill as a sommelier and noting that his palate was good as were his tasting abilities.

6) The horse ran past the barn fell.

   Correct as is.

   This sentence could be confusing and hinges on the adverb "past" which incidentally is the same as an adjective. Here, "ran" is used as a transitive verb (requiring the object "horse") but your first thought might have been to read "ran" as an intransitive verb (requiring no object i.e., I ran). Instead, the sentence means, "the horse that was run past the barn fell."

7) I have not studied late much *lately.*

   Lately modifies "have not studied" and needs to be an adverb.

8) *Late* as it was, I didn't mind being awoken by the clatter, for it meant that my wife had returned safely.

   "Late" is referring to the time, and is not modifying "was" therefore it should be an adjective

9) The mattress was *hard,* so the orthopedists agreed it was far superior to the soft one in preventing lower back pain.

   "Hard" is modifying mattress, not "was," so it should be an adjective not an adverb.

10) Because she is working so *hard* she will most likely not have time for dining with us, which is unfortunate because I have prepared her favorite

This is an interesting case: hard is modifying "working," which is a verb, so it must be an adverb. "Hard" actually is an adverb despite not ending in LY. "Hardly" is also an adverb, but it means "scarcely." In the context, we want to show that the woman is working intensely, not scarcely.

11) Because she is working *hardly* she will most likely have time for dining with us, which is fortunate, because I have prepared her favorite.

This is a context test: she is scarcely working, so she'll have time for dinner. "Scarcely" and "hardly" mean the same things.

12) If you stand up too fast you will develop lightheadedness and risk falling down.

Correct as is.

Fast is an adverb in this context. Be careful though, as "fast" can also be an adjective (i.e. "leading a fast life")

13) To reach the oil will require not only extensive surveys by geologists but digging deeply by miners.

Correct as is.

Arguably, this is a violation of parallelism, but there is no adjective/adverb error here. The miners will need to dig deep into the ground or "dig deeply."

14) The reason we go downtown and to flea markets is in order to purchase things like scarves and rugs *cheaply*.

"Cheaply" is modifying "purchase." To use "cheap" as an adjective it should come right before a noun (i.e. "a cheap dress")

15) She bakes miraculously well, and resultantly, her most recent creation tastes *amazing*.

Amazing is referring to the creation. To say her creation "tastes amazingly" implies that her creation has a refined palate capable of tasting things adroitly.

16) Though you may disagree with the adoption of the new core standards, you cannot refute that they were designed *specially* for the district by the director of the Department of Education.

Arguably this is a word-choice-error ("specially" could be traded for "especially"), but it is an adjective/adverb error as well.

Specially is modifying how the curriculum was designed.

17) Pensive, the man considered his options and mulled their consequences.

Correct as is.

"Pensive" is a modifier, giving us more information about the man.

18) Pensively, the man considered his options and mulled their consequences.

Correct as is.

"Pensively" is a modifier expressing now how the man considered his options.

19) When you go fishing, if you catch an *incredible*, rare tuna you would do well to put it back in the ocean.

-or-

When you go fishing, if you catch an *incredibly* (drop the comma) rare tuna you would do well to put it back in the ocean.

The issue here is when you have a comma after an adjective, then it requires another adjective to follow (i.e. a beautiful, wise, old man) and it follows the conventions of commas in lists.

A comma after an adverb follows the convention of standard comma usage (separating clauses or modifying expressions). But in the original sentence, the comma follows neither of these conventions.

20) When you go fishing, if you catch an *incredibly* rare tuna you would do well to put it back in the ocean.

Here is the case where an adverb is actually modifying an adjective. "Incredibly" is modifying "rare." If you wanted to say that the tuna was both incredible and rare, this would require a comma after "incredible."

21) Maybe they are unique and manufactured by that infamous three-named designer, but these *unbelievably* expensive shoes simply cannot be worth either the price or the death of the alligator that was required for their construction.

Just as in the case in number 20, "unbelievably" is modifying "expensive." Another fix would have been to place a comma after "unbelievable".

22) I must insist that if you structure your sentence like that, then your pronoun is being used wrong.

Correct as is.

It might sound better with "incorrectly" instead of "wrong" but "wrong" is both an adjective and an adverb.

23) The serenely flowing river passes by the resort and provides the perfect environment for men to fish, for women to sunbathe, and for families to recreate.

Again: an adverb modifying a noun. Here the noun is a special type called a gerund (the flowing river, the running man, the burning bush)

24) It was said of the spy that he conducted himself *ostentatiously*, and thus was the antithesis of what he needed to be.

"Ostentatiously" is modifying "conducted."

25) *Arguably* the best film of the year was the cartoon, which is unlikely to win any grand jury prizes, but will reside in the hearts and minds of the audiences for quite some time.

Despite being far from the verb, "arguably" is modifying "was."

26) In the space of the grand auditorium, and given the work that the benefactors had put into improving the acoustics so that the performances would resound better, the music sounds fully and *well*.

You're used to hearing that "music sounds good" meaning it is pleasing to the ear ("good" modifying the noun "music"). "Sound" is being used as an intransitive verb.

This example is referring to the process by which the music is being broadcast. "Sound" is being used as a transitive verb (i.e. to sound a bell, to sound out each letter). As such, "well" is modifying the verb "sound."

27) Funny enough, I was just mentioning to Sara last week that the way she walks is so staggeringly different from her sister's gait that it's hard to believe they're sisters.

Correct as is.

--or--

Funnily enough, I was just mentioning to Sara last week that the way she walks is so staggeringly different from her sister's gait that it's hard to believe they're sisters.

28) Funny enough, the comedian would serve the purpose for which we hired him: to provide some background entertainment as the guests arrived.

Correct as is.

This could NOT be changed to "funnily" as we're not describing how the comedian would serve.

29) I suppose that the moral of the story of the *Tortoise and the Hare* is that pacing oneself *slowly* and *steadily* wins the race.

Both adverbs describe "pacing."

30) It is arguable that the best film of the series will be the one produced most *inexpensively*, not the one which is an archetype of typical cinematic glut.

"Inexpensively" modifies "produced." Alternately, it would be acceptable to say, "...one produced, most inexpensive, and not the one..." but this makes less sense.

31) *Cinematically* showy movies are the stuff of awards shows and art house premiers, but I prefer a good cartoon any day.

"Cinematically" is modifying the adverb "showy"

32) Seemingly errant methods of calculating the sum of non-converging series can be deceptively simple but also deceptively complex if executed incorrectly.

"Seemingly" is modifying "errant"

33) *Obstreperously* well-meaning boys are not the norm at our institution, as we are more the type of school that takes demure, knowledge-seeking gentlemen.

"Obstreperously" is modifying the adjective phrase "well-meaning"

34) These errands are just eating away the daylight and my productivity, yet they are not *necessarily* the most important things I will do today, despite the hours they require of me.

"Necessarily" is modifying "are"

35) You cannot, nor should you try to fight the changing tide which so often overcomes us with its *insidiously* encroaching rhythms which placate us one moment and drown us the next.

"Insidiously" modifies the gerund "encroaching"

36) *Insufficiently* funded classes are one of the main reasons that schools in certain countries are at such a disadvantage relative to others.

"Insufficiently" modifies the adjective "funded"

37) Seek not to operate in a way that brings you happiness, for that is the goal of children, but to conduct yourself in a method that is *deliberately* angling you toward long term peace and the betterment of those around you.

"Deliberately" modifies "angling." It would also be appropriate to put a comma after "deliberate."

38) The pursuer is encouraged to send only one text message, to wait *patiently* until his text message is responded to, and then to respond in kind after an appropriate amount of time has lapsed, as to not seem too eager.

"Patiently" modifies the verb "wait."

39) The arbitrary arbiter, random and mercurial, *errantly*, albeit not without noble motives, decided to side with the plaintiff in the pollution case.

This is designed to trick you. You may be used to seeing adjectives in comma-separated lists and might have thought that "errant" was okay. But when you dissect the sentence, you see the first clause "random and mercurial" is a modifier which refers to "arbiter." "Errantly" is modifying "decided" and belongs to the second part of the sentence. If you dropped some of the adjectives, you could read the sentence as, "The arbiter errantly decided to side with the plaintiff."

40) A financial analyst, quantitatively-minded and good with computers, adroit, and with a strong fundamental knowledge of financial processes and valuations, is able to determine the value of equities and assign them relative ratings.

Correct as is. Also this would be grammatically correct to interchange "adroit" with "adroitly."

CHAPTER 2

Development and Organization

This is one of the easier things the SAT tests. While we tend to think of organization and flow as being subjective, in order for these topics to appear on a standardized test (like the SAT) they must follow rules.

And the rules we see applied are pretty straightforward.

When considering whether to insert a sentence, or the right order of sentences remember: every sentence needs to relate to what comes before it, and to what comes after it.

Pro Tip:

When considering the best way to join two sentences, look for the most concise version that

1) *Doesn't add any information*
2) *Doesn't delete any information*

The rest of this is common sense and logical argument progression, which for our purposes follows this structure:

Thesis/Intro:	new topic without too much specificity
Support:	specificity regarding the topic
Conclusion:	ending thoughts on the topic without opening a new line of inquiry

Practice

1 The 17th century was a period filled with near-constant war. **2** [1] Various cultural forces combined to create in northwestern Europe a climate of uncertainty and change. [2] At the same time, eastern Europe faced its own difficulties coming from Asia. [3] This was perhaps best illustrated in the Thirty Years' War, a destructive series of battles that ranged across present-day France, Switzerland, Germany, and Austria. [4] What started as a territorial battle between Protestant princes in the northern area of the Holy Roman Empire expanded into a conflict that involved the royal houses of Spain and France. **3** [5] Ultimately, the Thirty Years' War ended in the Peace of Westphalia, which established increased power for the regional Protestant rulers. **4** [6] In the latter case, Cardinal Richelieu exerted his significant power (he was the *de facto* ruler in place of the young King Louis XIV) in an effort to quell the expansion of Habsburg rule into the eastern portions of France. [7] The logical outcome of the intellectual side of the Protestant reformation was now somewhat complete; the ideas that had been expressed in local churches had reached the level of political power.

5 England was also a monarchy in the 1600s. As democratic feelings swept the island, Parliament attempted to impose its will on a variety of rulers from the House of Stuart, starting with James I and Charles I. **6** After a brief interlude in the middle of the century during which the country was ruled by Oliver Cromwell (who, born in 1599, lived most of the first half of his life in obscurity), the English appetite for a king proved too strong, and the latter part of the century saw the Stuarts reinstated through James II and Charles II. After repeated abuses, the English people invited William and Mary – from the nearby Netherlands - to be their king and queen. **7** From this point on, England became in effect a constitutional monarchy.

Spain's problems were more practical. In 1665, Charles II of Spain (of the House of Habsburg) ascended to the throne. Due to years of inbreeding, Charles was deformed, could barely speak, and suffered from emotional imbalances. **8** Against all conceivable odds, he ruled for 35 years, but he was never able to produce an heir. He named as his heir Philip, Duke of Anjou, himself of the ruling House of Bourbon in France. **9** [1] Phillip was a slight man with a variety of interests. [2] Thus, such a move represented a shift in power away from the House of Habsburg, which upset enough important statesmen in Europe so that it sparked another war, the War of Spanish Succession. [3] This war ended in a stalemate, as Philip was allowed to occupy the throne of Spain so long as he relinquished claims to the French throne. [4] Consolidation, whether by the Bourbons or the Hapsburgs, seemed impossible.

The most prominent figure of the 17th century lived in France, however. Louis XIV ruled for an astonishing 72 years, a time in which he was able to wed the traditions of French monarchy with the needs of modernity. He was a firm believer in the divine right of kings, and he ruled firmly and established a centralized state. **10** This state was powerful but ultimately unable to adapt to the needs of the day. During his time, French philosophy and literature underwent its own sort of renaissance. But Louis' most notable artistic achievement was his own home: the Palace of Versailles still stands as a testament both to the power and status of royals as well as the ingenuity of its architects. **11** In a time of regional volatility, Louis XIV – the "Sun King" – led France forward under the guide of his steady hand.

1) Which choice best introduces the main points expressed in the following paragraphs?
(A) NO CHANGE
(B) Few periods have seen such volatility as the 17th century.
(C) The Thirty Years' War ignited controversy across Europe.
(D) The 17th century was a period when a few important individuals shaped society.

2) For the sake of the cohesion of the entire essay, which sentence should be deleted?
(A) Sentence 1
(B) Sentence 2
(C) Sentence 3
(D) Sentence 4

3) The following addition would make most sense before sentence 3
(A) NO CHANGE
(B) Consequently,
(C) As a matter of fact,
(D) Therefore,

4) In order to maximize the logical flow of the first paragraph, sentence 6 should be placed
(A) Where it is now.
(B) After sentence 2.
(C) After sentence 3.
(D) After sentence 4.

5) Given the content of paragraphs 1 and 2, what is the best way to start paragraph 2?
(A) NO CHANGE
(B) England was definitely less volatile, however.
(C) But what was the true effect of the protestant reformation?
(D) England underwent its own transformations, as well.

6) Which of the following best stresses the tension between the people and their rulers?
(A) NO CHANGE
(B) a mysterious man who is difficult to describe
(C) a member of the well-respected gentry, but not a royal himself
(D) who himself had been influenced by the protestant reformation

7) Which choice, if added here, most effectively establishes the main change that occurs throughout the paragraph?
   (A) The move to look for a foreign ruler was an unprecedented one, but it was the only available option to a people who were fed up with the status quo.
   (B) After considering this offer for some time, William and Mary accepted.
   (C) This was done under the condition that their monarchy be a necessarily weak one.
   (D) Not all English people agreed with this, however, and some remained loyal to the Stuarts.

8) The underlined portion of this sentence should be revised to read:
   (A) NO CHANGE
   (B) Despite this
   (C) In addition
   (D) Therefore

9) To improve the focus of the paragraph, which sentence should be deleted?
   (A) Sentence 1
   (B) Sentence 2
   (C) Sentence 3
   (D) Sentence 4

10) In order to fulfill the ideas mentioned two sentences prior to this one, which is thc best choice?
   (A) NO CHANGE
   (B) Nevertheless, this state eventually crumbled and failed to serve its people.
   (C) However, he strove to move France out of its last vestiges of feudalism, and through his talented ministers, achieved prosperity for the state itself and its citizens.
   (D) This state was successful in that it took France back to a time when its people gladly served their king.

11) Which option best summarizes the final paragraph in the context of the essay at large?
   (A) NO CHANGE
   (B) Louis XIV effectively brought France into a new age and established himself as its greatest monarch.
   (C) Louis XIV's reign in effect silenced his Hapsburg critics and proved that the wars of the 17th century had been for naught.
   (D) In this way, Louis XIV proved himself to be a more effective leader than any of his contemporaries.

THE FOUNDING OF NEW ENGLAND

BY
JAMES TRUSLOW ADAMS

12 New England has always been an interesting place, but until it came under a single government, it was difficult to define. **13** [1] Not only are the boundaries between the six states which now form it negligible, but the section, as a whole, is a geographical unit, within which a common life, based upon generally similar economic, political, and religious foundations, has constituted a distinct cultural strain in the life of the nation. [2] The "New England idea" and the "New England type" have been as sharply defined as they have been persistent. [3] If, in our own day, they seem, to some extent, to be passing, their influence may be no less living because it is spread throughout the whole land, and absorbed into the common national life. [4] In this sense, New England is no longer a relevant concept.

14 [1] Diffusion over an unlimited space, in the one case, tends to weaken the hold on the land and the growth of the state, while, in the other, it greatly slows the development of those elements that make for civilized life. [2] Effective natural boundaries, defining a limited area, are of determining influence in fostering the life of primitive peoples or of civilized colonies. [3] It is noteworthy that, of the great river-highways leading to the interior of the continent — the St. Lawrence, the Hudson-Mohawk, and the Mississippi, — none was at first possessed by the English, who had everywhere, unwittingly but fortunately, selected portions of the coast where their natural tendency to expand was temporarily held in check. [4] Aside from other factors, the possession by the English, in the settlement period, of a limited and protected area, naturally restricted by the sea and the mountains, resulted, speaking broadly, in the building up of thickly settled, compact colonies as contrasted with the boundless empire of the French, opened to them by their control of the Mississippi and the St. Lawrence rivers.

12) Which of the following best introduces the main idea of the first paragraph?
(A) NO CHANGE
(B) Within the states of New England, it is tiny Rhode Island that stands out as the archetype of the region.
(C) The region of New England is not best defined as a geographical area but rather as a cultural idea.
(D) In the New England group we have one which, in spite of minor differences, is unusually homogeneous.

13) In order to clarify the purpose of the first paragraph, which sentence should be deleted?
(A) Sentence 1.
(B) Sentence 2.
(C) Sentence 3.
(D) Sentence 4.

14) Which ordering of sentences best establishes a logical flow to the second paragraph?

(A) 1, 2, 3, 4
(B) 2, 1, 4, 3
(C) 4, 3, 2, 1
(D) 3, 4, 1, 2

15 Certain names – in any field – are iconic. In physics: Albert Einstein. In painting: Michelangelo. In architecture: Frank Lloyd Wright. In music, the one name that stands out above all others in the 20th century is The Beatles. Despite the fact that we are less than one lifetime removed from the peak of The Beatles, it is easy to view them in an almost mythical way. **16** But to view the group as a simple archetype of greatness would miss a great deal; while The Beatles were legendary, they also had their weaknesses.

17 [1] The now-famous John, Paul, George, and Ringo were all born in the early 1940s in Liverpool, a bustling port city in northern England. [2] Northern England at the time was an area stuck between its rural traditions and a new industrial life. [3] In order to understand the beginnings of The Beatles, one must understand the reality of the city in which they grew up. [4] Liverpool was a working class city, the main point of access to northern England for the suppliers of many industries working in transatlantic trade. **18** [5] Thus, Liverpool came to serve dual roles: it was at once an industrial hub and a cultural epicenter. Local musicians so embraced the R and B infused rock music coming from American stars such as Elvis Presley and Buddy Holly that they created an entirely new music scene, Mersey Beat, named after the river that flows through Liverpool.

19 But Buddy Holly and Elvis Presley weren't the only two stars that The Beatles would come to idolize; many artists influenced the four young lads. **20** [1] A young John Lennon and Paul McCartney would sit together in their homes, trying to mimic the sounds that they heard on the latest "45s", small records with one or two songs on them. [2] Later, Paul brought his friend George along for an audition on the second level of a city bus. [3] At first, they failed, but over time they improved enough to be able to give small, impromptu performances at their school. [4] His rendition of popular song "Raunchy" earned him the instant respect of John, and what was a duo became a trio. **21** Finally, as the Beatles gained steam, they added fourth member Ringo Starr, himself already a bit of a local legend.

Like every band in the rock-saturated climate of Liverpool, The Beatles had to work hard for every gig, and soon their love of performance brought them to Hamburg, where they performed at the famous Cavern Club. These performances were less than glamorous, as the club is almost literally a cavern; the group performed in a small, brick recess of a basement dance floor. **22** Young and optimistic, they performed for up to six hours at a time. It was here, however, that The Beatles really started to come into their own.

When they returned to England, "Beatlemania" was in full force, and it soon spread to the United States. [1] After a 1964 performance on *The Ed Sullivan Show*, they were bona fide stars. **23** **24** [2] Throughout this time, The Beatles produced new music at a prolific rate, often seeing a new single replace their most recent hit as #1 on the charts. [3] An example of this is how "She Loves You" replaced "I Want to Hold Your Hand." [4] Their sound remained the same: short, jaunty tunes full of twangy guitars and vocal harmonies. [5] But just as the world began to feel comfortable with The Beatles' sound, they changed again, retiring from touring to focus on recording new albums. A trip to India resulted in spiritual reflection and the introduction of new instruments to their songs. The content of their songs now dealt with more than just teenage love, and their composition and recording methods changed as well. **25** In 1967, they released *Sgt. Pepper's Lonely Hearts Club Band;* the album cover artwork became almost as iconic as the band itself.

But as The Beatles' star rose, the stars that made up the group drifted apart. **26** Each member became his own entity that wished to flourish independently. By the time the groups recorded *Abbey Road* and *Let It Be,* the tension was palpable. A documentary film that accompanies the recoding of *Let It Be* shows not a group working cohesively, but instead friction between four different members. Towards the end of 1969, the group had effectively disbanded. This, however, was just the last step in what had been a ten-year evolution. **27**

15) Is the underlined sentence a good way to start the essay?
(A) No, because it distracts the reader from the main idea of the essay.
(B) No, because it sets up a comparison that the author doesn't complete.
(C) Yes, because it introduces several examples that the author develops throughout the essay.
(D) Yes, because it introduces several examples that the author uses to parallel his main subject.

16) Which choice best previews the ideas relayed in the rest of the passage?
(A) NO CHANGE
(B) The Beatles both struggled and evolved immensely in their ten years together.
(C) The recordings of The Beatles reveal a great inner struggle.
(D) Only after travelling around Europe did The Beatles acquire their signature sound.

17) For the sake of the cohesion of the paragraph, which sentence should be deleted?
(A) Sentence 1.
(B) Sentence 2.
(C) Sentence 3.
(D) Sentence 4.

18) Which sentence should be inserted here to best link sentences 4 and 5?
(A) But for all of Liverpool's blue-collar work ethic, its people longed for an escape.
(B) It was on ships coming from America that records of the new emerging sound – rock and roll – were imported and handed off to Britain's youth.
(C) The future would show, however, that these industrial suppliers would soon dwindle under less than perfect economic conditions.
(D) The journey across the Atlantic being so long led these sailors to listen to a lot of music on their journeys.

19) Which sentence best serves as a segue from the prior paragraph and previews the ideas in the rest of the essay?
   (A) NO CHANGE
   (B) John and Paul were the first of The Beatles to meet, and they developed a strong friendship.
   (C) It was in this environment that the member of The Beatles formed their musical identities, first separately, and then together.
   (D) Delete the entire sentence.

20) Which ordering of sentences is best for maintaining clarity and flow?
   (A) 1, 2, 3, 4
   (B) 2, 1, 3, 4
   (C) 1, 2, 4, 3
   (D) 1, 3, 2, 4

21) Which choice best finalizes the paragraph?
   (A) NO CHANGE
   (B) It would take some time until the trio became a quartet.
   (C) The Beatles soon recorded "Raunchy" and had a minor success with it.
   (D) George turned out to be a late bloomer, but he eventually complemented John and Paul well.

22) Which of the following is the best way to rephrase the underlined portion of the sentence?
   (A) NO CHANGE
   (B) Cramped and sweating,
   (A) Nervous and excited,
   (B) Shy and bashful,

23) Which sentence, if inserted here, best lends support to the claim made in sentence 1?
   (A) Still, no one would every quite surpass Elvis.
   (B) Feature films and sold-out concerts followed in due course.
   (C) They went from virtual unknowns to household names in the snap of a finger.
   (D) Music critics praised their technique and song composition.

24) To improve focus, which sentence should be deleted from this paragraph?
   (A) Sentence 2.
   (B) Sentence 3.
   (C) Sentence 4.
   (D) Sentence 5.

25) Which of the following best completes the preceding paragraph?
   (A) NO CHANGE
   (B) Probably the band's pinnacle achievement, the album made all of the band members proud.
   (C) The music on this record was virtually unrelated to their earliest recordings.
   (D) Ironically, a cardboard cutout of Elvis was featured on the cover of the album.

26)
   (A) NO CHANGE
   (B) In fact, the bands members literally moved away from each other, out into the London suburbs.
   (C) The band simply stopped functioning as a working unit.
   (D) Constant bickering threatened to ruin the legacy of the band.

27) Suppose the author wishes to contextualize the Beatles breakup within the themes of the entire passage and also end on an optimistic note. Which answer choice best achieves these goals?
   (A) The members of The Beatles were much happier after they broke up!
   (B) The breakup of The Beatles was not so much the end of a career as it was the start of four new ones.
   (C) The evolution that had seen ups and downs was unfortunately ending at a low point.
   (D) The Beatles brought many fans a great amount of joy during their ten-year careers.

28 Charles Dickens' *A Tale of Two Cities* provides an interesting introduction to the main themes of the French Revolution. But the novel is not historical fiction, per se, as certain liberties are taken in the recounting of events, and the book has all the trappings of Dickens' other novels, taking great care to craft memorable and intricate characters. **29**

30 [1] In one poignant scene, a nobleman, the Marquis de St. Evremonde, drives his carriage much too quickly through a crowded street, striking and killing a peasant boy. [2] It is the eve of the French Revolution, and while France enjoyed a place of great importance in the world, its successes were not equally shared amongst its people, and peasants in particular felt a rage at the ruling aristocracy. [3] With these iconic words, Dickens opens his novel with a description of the setting. [4] "It was the best of times, it was the worst of times…" [5] He dismissively tosses a gold coin at the boy's father, as if in recompense. While this act in itself wouldn't be overly odd, the reaction is: the coin is thrown back at the marquis as he drives away, enraging him, but more importantly, illustrating the mutual hostility between the aristocracy and the commoners. **31** It is this conflict that inspires the central plot of the novel.

Next we have a dramatic rendition of the storming of the Bastille, during which the French people invaded the prison in which so many political dissidents were housed. **32** This represented a remarkable victory for the people, and soon they would continue their progress. **33** [1] Soon, Louis XVI and his wife, Marie Antoinette, were themselves held in the Bastille before being executed at the guillotine. [2] Of course, it wasn't all rosy from here, and Dickens recounts with alacrity the ensuing reign of terror, when Maximillien Robespierre – a powerful dissident – took hold of the new French Republic and attempted to execute anyone who didn't agree with his extreme populist views. [3] History would ultimately judge Robespierre negatively, as an overzealous revolutionary who let his emotions get the better of him. [4] This time also came to an end, and Robespierre himself was executed in Paris' Place de La Revolution. **34**

35 With Robespierre gone, Dickens is finally able to focus on his character development. **36** [1] Darnay holds his own secrets, as he is the only son of the hated Marquis de Evremont. [2] There is his innocent and lovable daughter, Lucy, who eventually falls in love with Charles Darnay. [3] The book starts with the reclusive Dr. Manette, a Bastille prisoner serving time for a crime he cannot remember. [4] Realizing the wickedness of the house he is born into, Darnay tries to start a new life with a new name, but a pair of amoral spies threaten to reveal his family history. Then there are the Defarges, who from their Paris wine shop plot the machinations that will lead to the revolution. **37** In one important early scene, a cask of wine breaks, flooding the streets with what appears to be blood.

But the most important character is arguably Sydney Carton, who had previously led a life with little purpose or value. He falls in love with Lucy, which inspires him to reform himself; nevertheless, his love is never reciprocated. **38** Encouraged, he promises to do anything he can to secure her happiness. **39** [1] Darnay and Lucy eventually grow close and become engaged, and Carton's chance to be of help comes in the most dramatic way. [2] Darnay – who was never able to completely escape his past – is thrown in the Bastille during the reign of terror due to his familial associations. [3] Carton, who resembles Darnay physically, sneaks into the prison, replaces Darnay, and takes his place at the guillotine. [4] The glistening silver of the guillotine scares Carton, but he is able to keep his composure. Carton's final thoughts before he is executed are the stuff of legend: "It is a far, far better thing that I do, than I have ever done; it is a far, far better rest that I go to than I have ever known."

With this, *A Tale of Two Cities* comes to a close. **40** Dickens' focus on an accurate portrayal of the French Revolution resulted in both an exciting and educational read.

28) Which choice best introduces the topics outlined in the rest of the essay?
   (A) No Change.
   (B) As any critic or book-lover will tell you, *A Tale of Two Cities* is a classic of British literature.
   (C) Charles Dickens' *A Tale of Two Cities* has long been mischaracterized as historical fiction.
   (D) Of all of Dickens' novels, *A Tale of Two Cities* stands pre-eminent amongst the others as a masterpiece.

29) Which sentence – if added here – most effectively transitions to the next paragraph?
   (A) These ideas are perhaps best epitomized by the opening line of the book.
   (B) But characters can only get a book so far, and we will eventually come to see that the plot of *A Tale of Two Cities* is more important.
   (C) Even Dickens himself regarded this as one of his best novels.
   (D) (Do not add any sentence.)

30) Which ordering of sentences best preserves the logical flow of the paragraph?
   (A) 1, 2, 3, 4, 5
   (B) 2, 3, 1, 4, 5
   (C) 4, 3, 2, 1, 5
   (D) 5, 1, 2, 3, 4

31) Which choice best finishes the paragraph and establishes the link between Dickens' characters and the events of the French Revolution?
   (A) No change.
   (B) With this one dramatic scene, Dickens sows the seeds of discord that were present in late 18th-century France.
   (C) Will the commoners win in the end, or will the marquis' station in life insulate him from their rage? Only time will tell.
   (D) These sorts of conflicts occur more and more frequently until they boil over into the French Revolution.

32) Which choice best contextualizes the events in the previous sentence and qualifies their importance?
   (A) No change.
   (B) These prisoners were released and soon returned to normal lives.
   (C) This achievement was significant in that the Bastille was the most centralized location that the commoners had won.
   (D) This was a sort of symbolic victory that more or less pushed out the aristocracy.

33) Which of the following is the best way to rephrase the underlined portion of the sentence?
   (A) NO CHANGE
   (B) Therefore,
   (C) Lastly,
   (D) However,

34) To improve the focus of the paragraph, which sentence should be deleted?
(A) Sentence 1.
(B) Sentence 2.
(C) Sentence 3.
(D) Sentence 4.

35) Which of the following best marks a transition from a discussion of the events of the French Revolution to the particular skills of Dickens?
  (A) NO CHANGE
  (B) None of this is news to any student of French history, though, and Dickens' true gift is to build sub-plots and relatable characters that bring the events of the French Revolution to life.
  (C) From here, the French people themselves start to take on the qualities of a classic Dickensian character.
  (D) The Place de Revolution becomes a central setting for Dickens' novel, as well.

36) Which ordering of sentences best preserves the logical flow?
  (A) 1, 2, 3, 4
  (B) 4, 3, 1, 2
  (C) 3, 2, 1, 4
  (D) 3, 4, 1, 2

37) Which choice best lends support to the previous sentence?
  (A) No change.
  (B) Madame Defarge is a particularly ruthless individual: in her knitting, she writes in code the names of those aristocrats whom she wishes to execute.
  (C) The Defarges are a morally ambiguous couple: up until the end of the novel, we don't know if they are a force for good or for evil.
  (D) The Defarges, however, are not the only family with a stake in the outcome of the revolution.

38) Which of the following is the best way to rephrase the underlined portion of the sentence?
  (A) No change
  (B) Disheartened,
  (C) Devastated,
  (D) Unperturbed,

39) In order to improve the focus of the paragraph, which sentence should be deleted?
  (A) Sentence 1.
  (B) Sentence 2.
  (C) Sentence 3.
  (D) Sentence 4.

40) Which choice best summarizes the main ideas of the passage?

(A) A fine-toothed examination of the nature of literature in the zeitgeist of the respective authors.

(B) For all of its focus on the emotions of its characters, *A Tale of Two Cities* still manages to mention in passing a few of the more important events of the French Revolution.

(C) Through the use of sympathetic and nuanced characters, Dickens mirrors the events and themes of the French Revolution, bringing these historical events to life in an engaging way.

(D) Two great and iconic quotations bookend this modern classic.

Answers

1) The answer is B
   A is wrong because the passage does not focus solely on war, and the term "near-constant" is not supported by the passage. C is too specific; the passage mentions many other facets of the 17th-century other than the Thirty Years' War. D is wrong because while the passage does mention several important individuals, it also stresses cultural forces. B is the correct answer because the overall theme that the passage stresses is volatility and people's and nations' responses to it.

2) The answer is B.
   Eastern Europe has nothing to do with the rest of the paragraph or essay.

3) The answer is A.
   The sentence talks about the end of the war, which fits with the definition of the word "ultimately."

4) The answer is D.
   Sentence 6 talks about France and starts with the phrase "in the latter case." Sentence 4 ends with "Spain and France". Therefore, it makes sense to put sentences 6 directly after sentence 4.

5) The answer is D.
   A is wrong because the subsequent paragraph doesn't stress that England was a monarchy; it stressed how England changed. B is wrong because it doesn't seem to be true based on the information that is given in the second paragraph. C is wrong because that question is never answered or addressed. The correct answer is D. The first paragraph talks about the changes going on in continental Europe, and the second paragraph discusses changes in England.

6) The answer is C.
   A and B are wrong because they don't stress tension, as the question requests. D could be correct, but the question wants tension between the people and their rulers, and the best way to illustrate that is by stressing that Cromwell was not a royal, which made his ascendency to rule England all the more unusual and dramatic.

7) The answer is C.
B is wrong because it deals with William and Mary's inner thoughts and has nothing to do with England, per se. D is wrong because it stresses that some people wanted the status quo, while the questions asks us to "effectively establish the main change." A is close, but the second half of it may be an exaggeration. Was it their only option? Furthermore, the main change that the second paragraph mentions is a movement towards more democracy. This fits with answer choice C, which leads well into the final sentence of the paragraph.

8) The answer is B
The previous sentence emphasizes Charles' weaknesses, while this sentence mentions his long reign, so we need a phrase to establish change of direction. Answer B does this nicely. Answer A is the right idea, but it goes a little too far and is not consistent with the tone of the rest of the passage.

9) The answer is A
Sentences 2, 3, and 4 are all relevant to the action in Spain at the time and to the broader themes of the passage. Phillip's interests are not relevant to us, so we should delete sentence 1; the answer is A.

10) The answer is C
The previous two sentences state that Louis established a strong state but "wed [it] with the needs of modernity." A and B imply that the state was unsuccessful, which is not supported by the previous two sentences. D says that Louis took France backwards, which contradicts the "modernity" quote. C is a nice reflection of the way that Louis guided both the French people and the state itself.

11) The answer is A.
B is troubling because we don't know if Louis was France's "greatest" monarch. C is wrong because we don't know the reaction of his critics, and nowhere in the essay was it established that the wars were fought for no reason. D is wrong because we don't know enough about all of his contemporaries. The answer is A because the first part of the essay is about volatility and the second part stresses Louis' success in the face of it.

12) The answer is D
The first paragraph stresses the unity of New England. Answer choice D reflects this well.

13) The answer is D
Sentence 4 dismisses New England as unimportant and uninteresting, which contradicts the idea of devoting an entire paragraph to it. Answer D is correct.

14) The answer is B
Paragraph 1 emphasizes the unity of New England. Sentence 2 talks about how effective natural boundaries, which mirrors the idea of a unitary identity, are. Start paragraph 2 with sentence 2. Sentence 1 plays off of sentence 2 by giving the alternative scenario: "diffusion over an unlimited space." Put sentence 1 next. Finally, sentences 3 and 4 give examples of diffuse settlements (the French) and well-defined ones (the English), respectively. Since our new ordering of the first two sentences mentions well-defined settlements first and then diffuse ones, flip sentences 3 and 4. The answer is B.

15) The answer is D
The sentence is an effective way to introduce the next three sentences because it alerts the reader that the author is highlighting iconic names. However, the author never develops the next three example, so C is wrong. Answer D works well, since those three examples are "parallel" to The Beatles in that they are all iconic.

16) The answer is B
A is wrong because the passage doesn't really focus on any real weaknesses in the group. C is wrong because the focus of the passage is not on the recordings of The Beatles. D is simply an incorrect fact, and The Beatles' European travels are only mentioned in one paragraph. The passage is about how The Beatles changed over their time together, and it mentions some struggles, so answer choice B is correct.

17) The answer is B
The fact that northern England was stuck between rural traditions and new industrial life has no bearing on the essay. Delete sentence 2, and answer choice B is correct.

18) The answer is B
Sentence 4 mentions transatlantic trade, and sentence 5 mentions it as a "cultural epicenter." Why did this happen? Because through the transatlantic trade came music from America. Answer choice B is correct.

19) The answer is C
The rest of paragraph 3 doesn't mention any other influences on The Beatles, so A is wrong. B could work, but the second sentence mentions John and Paul by their full names, which it wouldn't do if they were already introduced by first-name only in the previous sentence. C works nicely because it acknowledges the ideas in the previous paragraph while previewing that the next paragraph will be about how The Beatles came together. Answer C is correct.

20) The answer is D
The first two Beatles to join each other were John and Paul, so 1 is a logical first sentence. Sentence 3 says "they failed," which seems to refer to John and Paul's attempts to mimic the sounds of new records. Put that sentence next. Sentence 4 says "his rendition," which can only apply to George, so sentence 2 must come before sentence 4. Thus, use 1, 3, 2, 4, which is answer choice D.

21) The answer is A
After this paragraph, the passage shifts its focus away from the formation of the band, so we should include any additions that we need to make. Answer choice A does this.

22) The answer is B
The previous sentences stress that the conditions in which The Beatles performed were less than ideal. Answer choice B reflects this.

23) The answer is B
The first sentence says they were "bona fide stars." A is wrong because it weakens their star power. D is wrong because it has nothing to do with being popular stars. C is close, but it doesn't really lend support to the previous statement, it just re-states the same idea. What might bona fide stars do? Star in films and give sold-out concerts. Answer choice B is correct.

24) The answer is B
Nowhere else in the essay is a specific song mentioned. Sentence 3 is a correct fact, but it's overly detailed for the scope of the essay, which focuses on the general arc of The Beatles' career. Answer choice B is correct.

25) The answer is C
This contrasts well with the previous statement that The Beatles' sound remained somewhat constant, and it helps establish the theme of the essay: that The Beatles evolved.

26) The answer is C
B is overly literal, C is factually incorrect, as the band did produce a few more albums, and nowhere is it implied that any disagreements ever threatened the band's legacy. Each member wanting to pursue his own interests fits well with "stars drifting apart." Answer choice C is correct.

27) The answer is B
The whole passage is about evolution. Since the questions asks us to use the themes of the passage but also be optimistic. Answer choice B is correct. It reframes a potentially sad event into a positive change.

28) The answer is A
B is overly speculative ("any critic"). C is overly critical. D implies that other of Dickens' novels are not masterpieces, which is not implied by the passage. A is a good overview of part of the essay and sets up a minor but appropriate contrast with the next sentence. Answer choice A is correct.

29) The answer is D
B sets up a prediction ("the plot is more important") that is never explicitly established. Nowhere else in the essay are Dickens' views mentioned, so C is mostly irrelevant. A is potentially correct, but it would be inappropriate to include A and then include a paragraph break before repeating the opening lines. There is really no need for an additional transition here. Answer D is correct.

30) The answer is C
Sentence 4 contains the opening words of the novel. That's a good place to start. Sentence 3 references "these iconic words," so put that next. Sentence 3 ends with "...description of the setting." Sentence 2 establishes this setting ("eve of the French Revolution"), so put that next. Sentences 1 and 5 give – in that order – a more specific example of the tension. The correct order is 4, 3, 2, 1, 5. Answer C is correct.

31) The answer is B
The question references both Dickens' characters and the events of the French Revolution. A doesn't address the revolution. C only addresses specific characters. D is close, but it's a little too focused on the reality of the 18th century. B mentions Dickens' skills ("one dramatic scene… sows the seeds") and references how they are linked to the genesis of the French Revolution. Answer B is correct.

32) The answer is D
The question asks to "qualify" the importance of the events in the previous sentence. To "qualify" means to contextualize or weaken the importance of. The only answer choice that does this is answer choice D, which references a "symbolic victory."

33) The answer is A
Answer choice A fits the idea that the storming of the Bastille led quickly to the capture of Louis and Marie.

34) The answer is C
Sentence 3 veers off into how historians judge Robespierre, and this essay is not precisely historical in nature. It also analyzes Robespierre as having "let his emotions get the better of him," which seems like speculation and is a departure from the tone of the rest of the essay.

35) The answer is B
The question asks for "the particular skills of Dickens". A and B are the only sentences that include a reference to Dickens' skills, but there's nothing about Robespierre being gone that would magically enable Dickens to finally focus on his characters. B does a good job acknowledging that while A Tale of Two Cities is set in an accurate historical setting, it is not groundbreaking history, per se, and then mentions what Dickens' skills are. Answer B is correct.

36) The answer is C
Sentence 3 opens with "The books starts with…" Let's put that first. Sentence 3 mentions Dr. Manette, and sentence 2 introduces his daughter, so let's put that next. Sentence 2 ends with introducing Darnay; let's put sentence 1 next because it gives more information about Darnay. Sentence 4 discusses the "wickedness of the house," which is a reference to the Marquis from sentence 1, so we'll finish with that. The correct order is 3, 2, 1, 4, which is answer choice C.

37) The answer is B
The previous sentences mentions the Defarges "plotting the machinations" of the French Revolution. Answer choice B effectively establishes that Madame Defarge is literally planning the demise of the aristocrats who will be the victims of the revolution.

38) The answer is D
The previous sentence mentions that Carton's love is not reciprocated, so A doesn't make any sense. B and C are negative, but Carton's actions suggest that he is not altogether depressed; he still wants to serve Lucy. "Unperturbed" means "unbothered by a bad situation," which fits his state of mind. Answer D is correct.

39) The answer is D
The focus of the passage is on how Carton serves Darnay and Lucy. Sentence 4, while relevant to the action, focuses solely on Carton's feelings. The answer is D.

40) The answer is C
The theme of the passage is that Dickens is able to wed his intricate characters and plot with some major historical events. B is dismissive of the latter because it says "in passing." D is overly specific; the focus of the essay was not the quotes. A fails to appreciate the unique skills that Dickens brought to this endeavor. C is equally respectful of the characters Dickens created and of the true-to-life events, and it explains the artistic link between them. Answer C is correct.

CHAPTER 3

Effective Language Usage

Effective Language Use tests us on our ability to critique the non-grammatical components of an author's work. Students are often intimidated because it reminds them of analyzing poetry and other exercises which have no objectively right answer. But, of course, in order for the SAT to remain a standardized test, the questions asked in this section all have clear, singular, right answers.

This section deals with the following: precision, concision, style, tone, syntax.

Three of those are basic.

- Precision: eliminate ambiguity.
  - Incorrect: *I want to go there.*
  - Correct: *I want to go to Texas.*
- Concision: use as few words as possible.
  - Incorrect: *And, therefore, understandably, and without question, the man said "no."*
  - Correct: *He of course said, "no."*
- Syntax: make sure your words are in the right order. English is a Subject Verb Object language. If you're curious as to what a syntax error looks like, think of anything Yoda from Star Wars would say.
  - Incorrect: *Go, you must. Stay here, you cannot.*
  - Correct: *You must go. You cannot stay.*

The last two are slightly harder.

- Style: this is how an author makes a statement. If you want to say that a bicycle is red you can either say

Reporting Style:	*The bicycle was red.*
Narrative Style:	*That ruddy hue; the amber glow; I will never forget the depth of crimson that I saw when I cast gaze upon that cycle.*
Opinion Style:	*I thought it was the most gorgeous red bicycle that I had ever seen.*

Whichever style the author uses, make sure all sentences are consistent with this style.

Pro Tip:

Style boils down to a few categories: opinion, reporting, or narrating. If the author is consistently using a reporting style ("The bicycle was red, had pedals, and was parked just outside of the school") then it is not appropriate for the author to switch to a narrative style ("And when Billy jumped on it, he remembered his youth: the fire trucks he would try to race, and the girls he'd try to impress") or an opinion style ("And I believe it was just about the best bicycle in the world).

- Tone: tone is the answer to the question: what is the author's attitude toward this topic.

Pro Tip:

Tone on the SAT is very limited. This is a very politically correct test. Authors will rarely be on the extremes. The SAT would not use an author who is vehemently approving nor one that is scornfully condemning. It is more likely to use authors whose tone is academic, removed, or considerate.

Practice

Answer the questions that follow the passages.

Passage I

Charles Darwin. The Descent of Man. 1871.

He [1] who wishes to decide whether man is the modified descendant of some pre-existing form, would probably first [2] enquire[1] into whether man varies, however slightly, in bodily structure and in mental faculties; and if so, whether the variations are transmitted to his offspring in accordance with the laws which prevail with the lower animals. Again, are the variations the result, as far as our ignorance permits us to judge, of the [3] same types of general causes, and are they governed by the same general laws, as in the case of other organisms; for instance, by correlation, the inherited effects of use and disuse, etc.?

....

The enquirer would next come to the [4] pretty major point, whether man tends to increase at so rapid a rate, as to lead to occasional severe struggles for existence; and consequently to beneficial variations, whether in body or mind, being preserved, and injurious ones eliminated. Do the races or species of men, whichever term may be [5] applied, encroach on and replace one another, so that some finally become extinct? [6] I believe that all these questions, as indeed is obvious in respect to most of them, must be answered in the affirmative, in the same manner as with the lower animals. But the several considerations just referred to may be conveniently deferred for a time: and we will first see how far the bodily structure of man shows traces, more or less plain, of his descent from some lower form. In [7] consecutive chapters the mental powers of man, in comparison with those of the lower animals, will be considered.

[1] "enquire" is the British spelling of "inquire"

Passage I

1) (A) NO CHANGE
(B) That
(C) Which
(D) Whom

2) (A) NO CHANGE
(B) Enquire about
(C) Enquire as to
(D) Enquire

3) (A) NO CHANGE
(B) Similar types of general causes
(C) Same general causes
(D) Similar general causes

4) (A) NO CHANGE
(B) Definitely major point
(C) Important point
(D) Totally important point

5) (A) NO CHANGE
(B) Implied
(C) Appropriated
(D) Implicated

6) (A) NO CHANGE
(B) We shall see that all these questions, as indeed is obvious in respect to most of them, must be answered in the affirmative.
(C) I believe that an affirmative answer to all these questions, as indeed is obvious in respect to most of them, is necessary.
(D) We shall see that all these questions, it is obvious, must be answered in the affirmative in respect to most of them.

7) (A) NO CHANGE
(B) Consequential
(C) Sequential
(D) Succeeding

Passage II

Hans Christian Andersen "What the moon saw" 1840

It is a strange thing, when I feel most fervently and most deeply, my hands and my tongue seem alike tied, so that I cannot **8** surely describe or accurately portray the thoughts that are rising within me; and yet I am a painter; my eye tells me as much as that, and **9** all of the many of my friends who have seen my sketches and fancies say the same.

I am a poor lad, and live in one of the narrowest of lanes; but I do not want for light, as my room is high up in the house, with an extensive **10** advantage over the neighboring roofs. During the first few days I went to live in the town, I felt **11** obviously low-spirited and solitary enough. Instead of the forest and the green hills of former days, I had here only a forest of chimney-pots to look out upon. And then I had not a single friend; not one familiar face greeted me.

So one evening I sat at the window, in a desponding mood; and **12** presently I opened the casement[1] and looked out. Oh, how my heart leaped up with joy! Here was a well-known face at last—a round, friendly **13** globe, the face of a good friend I had known at home. In, fact, it was the **14** MOON that looked in upon me. He was quite unchanged, the dear old Moon, and had the same face exactly that he used to show when he **15** peered around through the willow trees on the moor. I kissed my hand to him over and over again, as he shone far into my little room; and he, for his part, promised me that every evening, when he came abroad, he would look in upon me for a few moments. **16** This promise he has faithfully kept, pitifully only staying such a short time when he comes. Whenever he appears, he tells me of one thing or another that he has seen on the previous night, or on that same evening. "Just paint the scenes I describe to you"—this is what he said to me—"and you will have a very pretty picture-book." I have followed his injunction for many evenings. I could make up a new "Thousand and One Nights," in my own way, out of these pictures, but the number might be too **17** many, after all. The pictures I have here given have not been chosen at random, but follow in their proper order, just as they were described to me. **18** Some great gifted painter, or some poet or musician, may make something more of them if he likes; what I have given here are only hasty sketches, hurriedly put upon the paper, with some of my own thoughts, interspersed; for the Moon did not come to me every evening— a cloud sometimes hid his face from me.

[2] "casement" refers to the hinge of a window

8) (A) NO CHANGE
(B) Certainly
(C) Rightly
(D) Comfortably

9) (A) NO CHANGE
(B) All
(C) The most of all
(D) Mostly of

10) (A) NO CHANGE
(B) Shadow
(C) Protection
(D) Prospect

11) (A) NO CHANGE
(B) Low-spirited
(C) Totally depressed
(D) Low-minded

12) (A) NO CHANGE
(B) Simultaneously
(C) Earlier
(D) At present

13) (A) NO CHANGE
(B) Countenance
(C) Ghost
(D) Eye

14) What tone does the author convey by capitalizing "MOON"?
(A) Disbelief
(B) Bewilderment
(C) Exuberance
(D) Contentment

15) (A) NO CHANGE
(B) Peered onto me
(C) Peered over me
(D) Peered down upon me

16) (A) NO CHANGE
(B) This promise he has faithfully kept, for it is a pity that he can only stay such a short time when he comes.
(C) This promise he has faithfully kept. It is a pity that he can only stay such a short time when he comes.
(D) It is a pity that he can only stay such a short time when he comes, though he has faithfully kept this promise.

17) (A) NO CHANGE
(B) Great
(C) Uninteresting
(D) Uncertain

18) Which of the following best describes the tone conveyed by the author by his use of the phrases: "Some great gifted painter… hurriedly put upon the paper"
(A) Embarrassment
(B) Apathy
(C) Self-Deprecation
(D) Realism

Passage III

Marion Meade. In Hollywood with Nathanial West. 2011.

Hollywood has served as **19** novelist's muses for almost a century. The list of writers who found inspiration there includes **20** those including Fitzgerald, Mailer, Schulberg, Bukowski, Chandler, Huxley, Waugh, and O'Hara, among plenty of others. But the **21** gold standard for Hollywood fiction remains *The Day of the Locust.*

Nathanael West—novelist, screenwriter, playwright—was one of the most original writers of his generation, a comic artist whose insight into the brutalities of modern life would prove remarkably prophetic. In addition to *The Day of the Locust* he is the author of another classic *Miss Lonelyhearts* (1933) as well as two minor works, *The Dream Life of Balso Snell* (1931) and *A Cool Million* (1934).

Seventy years after publication, *The Day of the Locust* is still **22** a super important Hollywood story. Beyond that, West's story examines America during the Great Depression, revealing a diseased country being stained by corruption, hypocrisy, greed, and rage.

Movie stars who get their faces on the screen did not excite West. Neither was he dazzled by Hollywood as the glitz and glamour capital of the world. Instead, his tale goes backstage to focus on the raw inner workings of a byzantine business and the working stiffs who write scripts, design sets, and appear in crowd scenes.

23 In the novel's opening scene, a mob of fake infantry and cavalry is being herded away to fight the fake Battle of Waterloo. "Stage Nine—you bastards—Stage Nine!" a second unit director shouts hysterically through his megaphone.

West's heroes are the cheated ones dredged up from the sea of extras and bit players, the **24** successful assistant directors and lowly writers. Buzzing in the background, meanwhile, are the locusts, the plagues of angry migrants disconnected from Middle America, seduced by the promise of California sunshine and citrus. (*The Grapes of Wrath* showcases some of the same displaced folks.) Battered by hard knocks, these ragtag bands hang out at movie premieres to **24** observe celebrities and sometimes they freak out and start busting balls for no apparent reason. In *The Day of the Locust*, they are first responsible for a bloody murder, then they riot and start setting fire to the city.

19) (A) NO CHANGE
(B) Novelists' muse
(C) A novelist's muse
(D) The muse of a novelist

20) (A) NO CHANGE
(B) The likes of
(C) Some writers such as
(D) Other writers like

21) What does the author's choice of the descriptor "gold standard" imply about "The Day of the Locust"?
(A) "The Day of the Locust" was the best work of its genre.
(B) "The Day of the Locust" was unique and difficult to imitate.
(C) "The Day of the Locust" was an expensive work to produce.
(D) "The Day of the Locust" turned a large profit.

22) Which phrase would best complete this sentence in keeping with the style of the article?
(A) NO CHANGE
(B) A fairly interesting novel.
(C) The most significant novel ever written about Hollywood.
(D) One of my favorite novels.

23) Do these two sentences support the author's argument? Why/Why not?
(A) Yes. They explain West's interest in tales of Hollywood movie stars.
(B) Yes. They serve an example of West's fascination with behind the scenes work.
(C) No. While they support the main argument, they are too detailed.
(D) No. These lines do not support the argument.

24) (A) NO CHANGE
(B) Prosperous
(C) Tiresome
(D) Menial

25) (A) NO CHANGE
(B) Gawk at
(C) Mingle with
(D) Befriend

Passage IV.

Thomas Bulfinch (1796–1867). Age of Fable: Vol. III: The Age of Chivalry. 1913.

King Arthur and His Knights

III. **Merlin**

MERLIN was the son of no mortal father, but of an Incubus, one of a class of beings not absolutely wicked, but far from good, **26** who inhabit the regions of the air. Merlin's mother was a virtuous young woman, who, on the birth of her son, entrusted him to a priest, who hurried him to the baptismal fount[1], **27** and so saved him from sharing the lot of his father, and consequently he retained many marks of his unearthly origin.

At this time Vortigern reigned in Britain. He was a **28** troublemaker, who had caused the death of his sovereign, Moines, and driven the two brothers of the late king, whose names were Uther and Pendragon, into banishment. Vortigern, who lived in constant fear of the return of the rightful heirs of the kingdom, began to erect a strong tower for defense. **29** The edifice, which fell three times to the ground when brought by the workmen to a certain height, without any apparent cause. The king consulted his astrologers on this wonderful event, and learned from them that it would be necessary to bathe the corner-stone of the foundation with the blood of a child born without a mortal father.

In search of such an infant, Vortigern sent his messengers all over the kingdom, and they by accident discovered Merlin, whose lineage seemed to point him out as **30** the individual that Vortigern wanted. They took him to the king; but Merlin, young as he was, explained to the king the absurdity of attempting to rescue the fabric by such means, for he told him the true cause of the **30** instability of the tower was its being placed over the den of two immense dragons, whose combats shook the earth above them. The king ordered his workmen to dig beneath the tower, and when they had done so they discovered two enormous serpents, the one white as milk the other red as fire. The **32** multitude looked on with amazement, till the serpents, slowly rising from their den, and expanding their enormous folds, began the combat, when every one fled in terror, except Merlin, who stood by clapping his hands and cheering on the conflict. The red dragon was **33** slayed, and the white one, gliding through a cleft in the rock, disappeared

[1] baptisimal fount is an article of church furniture or a fixture used for the baptism, mostly of small children but even older children, teenagers and adults.

26) (A) NO CHANGE
(B) That
(C) Whom
(D) Which

27) (A) NO CHANGE
(B) And so saved him from sharing the lot of his father, though he retained many marks of his unearthly origin.
(C) And so saved him from sharing the lot of his father. Therefore he retained many marks of his unearthly origin.
(D) And so saved him from sharing the lot of his father. He retained many marks of his unearthly origin.

28) (A) NO CHANGE
(B) Criminal
(C) Evildoer
(D) Usurper

29) (A) NO CHANGE
(B) The edifice, when brought by the workmen to a certain height, three times fell to the ground, without any apparent cause.
(C) Without any apparent cause, when brought by the workmen to a certain height, three times to the ground fell the edifice.
(D) The edifice, which when brought by the workmen to a certain height, without any apparent cause fell to the ground.

30) (A) NO CHANGE
(B) The individual that would be wanted
(C) The individual wanted
(D) The most likely individual to be wanted

31) (A) NO CHANGE
(B) Eeriness
(C) Squalor
(D) Haplessness

32) The use of the word "multitude" implies the presence of:
(A) Children
(B) Several onlookers
(C) A crowd
(D) Church officials

33) (A) NO CHANGE
(B) Slain
(C) Slay
(D) Slew

Olaus Magnus's Sea Serpent. Joseph Nigg.

In his comprehensive study, *The Great Sea-Serpent: An Historical and Critical Treatise* (1892), Dutch zoologist Antoon Cornelius Oudemans lists more than three hundred references to the **34** well-known sea monster in his chronological "Literature on the Subject." The first ten of those, 1555-1665, cites Olaus Magnus's sea serpent: editions of Olaus's *Historia de gentibus septentrionalibus* ("History of the Northern Peoples") and natural histories of Conrad Gesner, Ulisse Aldrovandi, Edward Topsell, and John Jonston. The list establishes Olaus's serpentine monster as the major ancestral source of sea serpent lore from the sixteenth century to widespread sightings of such creatures in Oudemans's own time. It is the basis for illustration and discussion of the creature in marine studies and popular fantasy up to the present, five hundred years after Olaus created it.

35 Oudemans cites natural histories in which copies or variations of Gesner's famous woodcut of Olaus's sea serpent appear. His list does not refer to the monster's iconic source: the 1539 *Carta Marina*. Oudemans had not seen the map. After it went out of circulation by the 1580s, it was lost for three centuries until a copy was discovered in the Munich state library in 1886, shortly before publication of *The Great Sea-Serpent*. A second copy surfaced in 1962 and is now in the Uppsala University Library. The wall map, **36** measuring about 5 feet (1.5m) wide and 4 feet (1.2m) high, was the largest, most accurate, and most detailed map of Scandinavia—or of any European region—at that time. A Catholic priest exiled with his Archbishop of Uppsala brother, Johannes, from their native Sweden after it converted to Lutheranism, Olaus began compiling the **37** nationalistic map in Poland in 1527. **38** The map was printed in Venice twelve years later. It was created to show the rest of Europe the rich history, culture, and natural wonders of the North prior to the Reformation.

The northern seas of the marine and terrestrial map teem with **39** large sea monsters either drawn or approved by Olaus. The most dramatic of those, off the busy coast of Norway, below the dreaded Maelström, is the great serpent, coiling around a ship's mast and lunging with bared teeth at a sailor on the deck. Like the map's other sea beasts, the serpent is not just a cartographical decoration to fill space, as in Jonathan Swift's "elephants in wont of towns." It is meant to represent a real animal, one that Nordic sailors and fishermen vividly described to Olaus on his travels around Scandinavia. **40** The Latin legend accompanying the image indicates the monster is 300 feet (91.4m) in length. According to the map's key, on the other hand, it is "A worm 200 feet long wrapping itself around a big ship and destroying it."

34) (A) NO CHANGE
(B) Popular
(C) Notable
(D) Notorious

35) Which of the following is the best combination of the two underlined sentences?

(A) Even though Oudemans cites natural histories in which copies or variations of Gesner's famous woodcut of Olaus's sea serpent appear, I believe his list

(B) While Oudemans cites natural histories in which copies or variations of Gesner's famous woodcut of Olaus's sea serpent appear, his list

(C) Oudemans cites natural histories in which copies or variations of Gesner's famous woodcut of Olaus's sea serpent appear because his list

(D) Oudemans cites natural histories in which copies or variations of Gesner's famous woodcut of Olaus's sea serpent appear, in spite of the fact that his list

36) Should the author include the underlined detail? Why/ Why not?

(A) Yes. The detail is necessary to prove that the map was the largest.

(B) Yes. The detail serves to impress and entertain the audience.

(C) No. The detail is not relevant to the main point of the sentence.

(D) No. The detail would be better included elsewhere in the paragraph.

37) By using "nationalistic", what characteristic does the author imply of Olaus?

(A) Close-minded

(B) Superiority

(C) Diligence

(D) Intelligence

38) (A) NO CHANGE

(B) The map was printed in Venice twelve years later in order to show the rest of Europe the rich history, culture, and natural wonders of the North prior to the Reformation.

(C) Created to show the rest of Europe the rich history, culture, and natural wonders of the North prior to the Reformation, the map was printed in Venice twelve years later.

(D) Created to show the rest of Europe the rich history, culture, and natural wonders of the North prior to the Reformation, in Venice twelve years later, the map was printed.

39) (A) NO CHANGE

(B) Realistic

(C) Supernatural

(D) Fantastic

40) Why does the author give two different accounts of the monster's length?
   (A) To show that, as a real animal, various descriptions have been recorded.
   (B) To emphasize how large the animal is.
   (C) To call the map's integrity into question.
   (D) To present a balanced account of all of the information on the map.

Answers

Passage I

1) (A) NO CHANGE
This is correct since "who wishes to decide" is the independent clause antecedent for "He".

2) (D) enquire
Enquire does not require any other preposition than "whether".

3) (C) same general causes
"Types of" is unnecessarily wordy. Similar is "resembling without being identical", while same is "identical; not different". Therefore, in this case the author is saying that the exact same causes are at work so "similar" is incorrect.

4) (C) important point
Do not use exaggerated language. The tone of this article is pedagogical.

5) (A) NO CHANGE
The definitions of the other sound-alike words do not fit the context.

6) (B)
We shall see that all these questions, as indeed is obvious in respect to most of them, must be answered in the affirmative
It is out of the style for the author to use "I believe". Answers C and D have convoluted sentence structure.

7) (D) succeeding
All terms relate to the order of the book chapters, however only succeeding meaning "following" fits in this context.

Passage II

8) (C) rightly
Use "accurately" as a guide. The correct answer is rightly, which is a synonym.

9) (D) mostly of
"all of the many of" and "the most of all" are too wordy, since they include several prepositional phrases. "Mostly of" is incorrect since mostly is an adverb. "Most of" could work, but it is not presented as an answer choice.

10) (D) prospect
Since his room is high and it has plenty of light, you can assume that he is higher than the neighboring roofs. Therefore, the correct answer is "prospect", meaning that he has a view of the roofs. This is substantiated by this segment of the last sentence of the paragraph: "I had here only a forest of chimney-pots to look out upon."

11) (B) low-spirited
"obviously" and "totally" are too informal and overly dramatic. Low-minded means vulgar, which is not indicated by the passage.

12) (A) NO CHANGE
From the sentence, infer that the author means that they opened the window AFTER they had been sitting in the window. Then "presently" is the only word that makes sense.

13) (B) countenance
Countenance is a synonym for face. The other words are too vague or slightly off-point.

14) (C) Exuberance
The author says his "heart leaped up with joy" indicating joy. The author does not indicate that he disbelieves or is bewildered by the situation. Contentment is not a strong enough word.

15) (D) peered down upon me
The meaning is that the moon is shining down onto the author.

16) (C) This promise he has faithfully kept. It is a pity that he can only stay such a short
time when he comes.
(A) is out because this would imply that the second clause depends on the first clause, when in actuality they contrast. (B) is out because the sentences cannot be joined by "for", as they contrast. (D) is out because the first sentence directly follows from the previous sentence, because it refers to "this promise".

17) (B) great
Context tells that there are many, many pictures "I have followed his injunction for many evenings", but "the number might be too many" is incorrect because "many" can only modify plural nouns that can be counted and "the number" is singular. (C) and (D) are testing the comprehension of the sentence.

18) (D) Realism
(A) and (C) are too extreme. (B) implies that he does not care about the work which is inaccurate, based on the passage. (D) is correct in the context of the passage.

Passage III

19) (B) novelists' muse
Multiple novelists (plural) use a single muse.

20) (B) the likes of
(A), (C) and (D) are all redundant, and (D) is also informal.

21) (A) "The Day of the Locust" was the best work of its genre.
This question requires the student to understand the use of the term "gold standard" which means: "The best or most prestigious thing of its type".

22) (C) the most significant novel ever written about Hollywood.
(A) is too informal. (B) and (D) inject personal opinion, whereas the rest of this piece is written in an educational style.

23) (B) Yes. They serve an example of West's fascination with behind the scenes work.
The previous part says that West focuses on the "inner workings" of movies. These lines are an example of how he does that.

24) (D) menial
Use "lowly" as a guide. The author is talking about people who are lower status. Prosperous and successful are synonyms. Tiresome means boring which is not the right meaning.

25) (B) gawk at
(A) is too mild, (C) and (D) do not make sense in context. Gawk at means stare at awkwardly, which fits.

Passage IV.

26) (A) NO CHANGE
This pronoun refers to a being rather than object, so it should be either who or whom. Who, the subjective form, is correct because "who inhabit" is of the form subject/verb.

27) (B) and so saved him from sharing the lot of his father, though he retained many marks of his unearthly origin.
(B) and (C) imply a cause and effect, but the relationship should be contrasted as shown in (B).

28) (D) usurper
Usurper specifically means one who takes the power of the thrown for himself illicitly.

29) (B) The edifice, when brought by the workmen to a certain height, three times fell to the ground, without any apparent cause.
All sentences contain misplaced modifiers except (B).

30) (C) the individual wanted
The other options are unnecessarily wordy or redundant.

31) (A) NO CHANGE
The falling of the edifice combined with the "shaking of the earth" indicates that the building was unstable. "eeriness" means handedness, "haplessness" not lucky, and squalor means state of being very dirty.

32) (C) a crowd
Multitude means a large crowd.

33) (B) slain
Slain is the correct past participle.

34) (D) notorious
Notorious is the only one that has a negative connotation, as is fitting for a sea monster.

35) (B) While Oudemans cites natural histories in which copies or variations of Gesner's famous woodcut of Olaus's sea serpent appear, his list
(A) "I believe" interjects personal opinion. (C) "because" includes causation which is incorrect. (D) is excessively wordy.

36) (A) Yes. The detail is necessary to prove that the map was the largest.

37) (B) Superiority
Nationalistic implies that Olaus was very proud of his country and believed it to be superior to other countries.

38) (C) Created to show the rest of Europe the rich history, culture, and natural wonders of the North prior to the Reformation, the map was printed in Venice twelve years later.

39) (D) fantastic
(A) is out because the size of the creatures was not mentioned. (B) is out because creatures were described as "dramatic" (C) is out because it also says that they were meant to represent real animals

40) (A) To show that, as a real animal, various descriptions have been recorded

CHAPTER 4

Faulty Comparisons

Faulty comparisons are the epitome of "but that sounds fine" errors. Faulty comparisons usually sound *better* in the incorrect version.

Incorrect: *The Mexican food in LA is so much better than Chicago.*
Correct: *The Mexican food in LA is so much better than the Mexican food in Chicago.*

The first sounds fine, looks fine, and makes sense. The second sounds a little wordy, but it's correct.

Once you see these the correction is simple. It's spotting the error that is the challenge.

Pro Tip:

The vast majority of time that the SAT compares anything in a sentence, it is doing so to test this error. Therefore, if you see two things being compared anywhere on the writing section, you should assume this error is being tested.

Practice

Most of the following sentences contain faulty comparisons. Identify those that do, and rewrite the proper comparison

1) This required more capital than initially estimated.

2) Even though a mockingbird is considered to be a weak, frail bird, its body structure is more muscular than the American eagle.

3) Educators would have us believe that there is this great disparity—that the way girls learn is far different from boys—but in reality, gender has a mind-numbingly small pull on the way two people will understand a topic.

4) Eagerly packing for his trip to Alaska, my friend included only warm-weather clothes, for after consulting a map he saw Alaska was placed right beside Hawaii, so he reasoned that the weather in Hawaii would be as warm if not cooler than Alaska due to their proximity on the map, but it was not until someone pointed out that Alaska was only placed near Hawaii to save space on the map that he realized the error of his ways.

5) Usury is a sin that has a particular place in Biblical history that somehow flowed through to modern day: the theory is that charging rates of interest that are higher than banks is a special kind of wrong.

6) The neophytes love to try to show off their knowledge of coffee by blurting out that coffee has a higher caffeine content than espresso, which is just outlandishly specious, and what they mean to say is that, coffee *per serving* (usually 8oz.) has more caffeine than espresso, whose serving size is two ounces.

7) The leader annexed the small outcropping from the country to whom he had given the parcel only 20 years earlier, not realizing that the oil fields he was seeking control over had far poorer yield projections than his own country.

8) Look at Jackson Pollock, and then look at the group known as The Old Masters, and try to tell me that the work hasn't progressed, or that the work of one is equal to the other.

9) While visiting Central America, we learned that twice as many bug species live along the equator than anywhere else in the world.

10) Jim, running unopposed for the Green party's presidential nominee, received understandably-more votes than did either the Republican or Democratic Party.

11) There's a conception that weather systems in enclosed waterways like the Great Lakes are less daunting than open waterways like the Atlantic Ocean, when really, per-square-mile the two have similar mortality rates.

12) Siskel and Ebert praised the new movie, saying that it was more thoroughly exciting and thought-provoking than any movie of that year.

13) If you decide someday that she was the one for you, and that she was better than any girl you had known, you run the risk that she will not be available to you at that time—that your timing will just not align.

14) Art classes in European classrooms, unlike American classrooms, often focus more on theory and appreciation than on actively creating art.

15) More and more, modern songwriters, like medieval composers, are opting for simplistic beats and melodies instead of overly complicated ones.

16) The air-conditioning units of new, "eco-friendly" homes are much cleaner and more efficient than older homes.

17) To music writers of the time, the songs of the The Beatles were as entertaining, if not more so, than Elvis.

18) In the modern world, unlike the past, people often communicate via the internet, and friends sometimes go long periods of time without seeing each other face-to-face.

19) Even today, in many parts of the world disabled people are treated like a burden, or worse yet, like a non-citizen.

20) Entertaining and throwing parties in the day is not at all like night when the natural energy levels mellow, people are more likely to imbibe, and the event naturally has an air of intrigue.

21) It is somewhat paradoxical that thriving at college is somewhat less difficult than in high school, as one is allowed to choose one's classes and therein is allowed to have a greater sense of fulfilled intellectual curiosity.

22) The athlete had a tremendous workout—running all the stairs in the stadium—but she was warned by her coach that if she continued this overtraining she would run the risk of doing more harm to her muscle groups than good.

23) Among those that play chess, the aforementioned player is by far the better.

24) Between those that play chess, the aforementioned player is by far the best.

25) Among my two brothers and I, my brother Ken is the obviously better cook.

26) Among the flautists, there are distinctions for first, and second-chair, and obviously the first-chair flautist is the best.

27) I began reading the essay expecting the usual drivel so common among middle-schoolers, but by the end I was very pleasantly surprised, and I would even say that it was the most perfect composition by someone of that age that I have ever seen.

28) Baseball statisticians are well-known and well-paid for tracking all the metrics of baseball players and for reporting back to management if, for example, one player scores more points than the last game.

29) I'm eighty-six next month while my wife is only seventy-nine, so I'm thinking that statistically she has more time to live than me.

30) I am less hungry than an hour ago, but I'm sure I'll get an appetite once we sit down to eat.

31) The analyst had a successful half-year review, and with his new salary, he was on target to earn more than last year.

32) At times, one has to wonder why people chose to inhabit Australia: started as a penal colony of the British, it is now home to a species of jellyfish whose venom is the only thing more poisonous than a bite by one of their legendary spiders.

33) Unlike those cheesy motivational posters, I would not advise you to simply "Do what you're passionate about" as you must do what is necessary, good, and lucrative, and this may not always tie in to what you're passionate about.

34) Similar to your relationship, an online dating site was where I found my current girlfriend.

35) In areas of strength, as in weakness, it is important to have perspective and realize that you are not the worst, nor the best, just another one trying to excel, fighting your own battles.

36) I encourage everyone to enjoy the ride, as we cannot be sure if any moment will be better than the last or worse than the prior.

37) When the FBI caught the man who had been hacking into the accounts of celebrities, he commented that it was interesting how all celebrities seemed to date one another, preferring perpetual change to any one person.

38) I was singularly unimpressed by the nominees this year, and found no one to be better than any of the nominees.

39) Earning one's fortune is far preferable to the lottery victory, as the former will provide you with a linear sense of success, while the latter will be like an explosion in your life.

40) In the tired and worn-out post-test phase of the six-hour exam, the candidates agreed that this year was far more challenging than the test of last year.

Answers

1) This required more capital than *was* initially estimated.
Otherwise you're comparing "capital" to "initially estimated."

2) Even though a mockingbird I considered to be a weak, frail bird, its body structure is more muscular than *that of* the American eagle.
Otherwise you're comparing "body structure" to "eagle."

3) Educators would have us believe that there is this great disparity—that the way girls learn is far different from *the way boys learn*—but in reality, gender has a mind-numbingly small pull on the way two people will understand a topic.

4) Eagerly packing for his trip to Alaska, my friend included only warm-weather clothes, for after consulting a map he saw Alaska was placed right beside Hawaii, so he reasoned that the weather in Hawaii would be as warm if not cooler than *that of* Alaska due to their proximity on the map, but it was not until someone pointed out that Alaska was only placed near Hawaii to save space on the map that he realized the error of his ways.
Without these two words, we're comparing weather in Hawaii to the state of Alaska.

5) Usury is a sin that has a particular place in Biblical history that somehow flowed through to modern day: the theory is that charging rates of interest that are higher than *those of* banks is a special kind of wrong.

-or-

Usury is a sin that has a particular place in Biblical history that somehow flowed through to modern day: the theory is that charging rates of interest that are higher than banks' is a special kind of wrong.
Note the apostrophe in the second correct version. Both revised versions grammatically shift the comparison from interest-rates-to-banks, to interest-rates-to-interest-rates.

6) The neophytes love to try to show off their knowledge of coffee by blurting out that coffee has a higher caffeine content than espresso, which is just outlandishly specious, and what they mean to say is that, coffee *per serving* (usually 8oz.) has more caffeine than espresso *per serving*, whose serving size is two ounces.
We must add the second "per serving" otherwise we're comparing "coffee per serving" to "espresso" which might seem correct, but is as erroneous as comparing "miles per hour" to "kilometers."

7) The leader annexed the small outcropping from the country to whom he had given the parcel only 20 years earlier, not realizing that the oil fields he was seeking control over had far poorer yield projections than *those of* his own country.
Again, the sentence hinges on those two words "those of" which redirects the comparison from errant to correct.

8) Look at Jackson Pollock, and then look at the group known as The Old Masters, and try to tell me that the work hasn't progressed, or that the work of one is equal to the *work of* other.

9) While visiting Central America, we learned that twice as many bug species live along the equator than *live* anywhere else in the world.

-or-

While visiting Central America, we learned that twice as many bug species live along the equator than *do* anywhere else in the world.
This is a very tricky question. As stated, it is so colloquially appropriate that it's hard to understand where it could be wrong. An analogous sentence that might help elucidate the error would be:

More people go to school than nine.

Clearly that is wrong. It's a little nonsensical either way, but if you say

More people go to school than are nine

It makes a little more sense: we're (for some reason) comparing the number of people who attend school to the number of people who are nine years old. Here, clearly we need the second verb "are" before "nine". Likewise in the sentence above, we need the verb "do" or "live" to properly structure the comparison.

10) Jim, running unopposed for the Green party's presidential nominee, received understandably-more votes than did either the Republican or Democratic *parties' candidates*.
This is tricky because you often hear of political parties receiving votes, and whether or not this is appropriate, the sentence starts by comparing the votes that Jim (a single person) received, so it is most appropriate to compare this to the votes that other candidates (not parties) received.

11) There's a conception that weather systems in enclosed waterways like the Great Lakes are less daunting than *those of* open waterways like the Atlantic Ocean, when really, per-square-mile the two have similar mortality rates.

12) Siskel and Ebert praised the new movie, saying that it was more thoroughly exciting and thought-provoking than any *other* movie of that year.
This is another form of the faulty comparison error that we've not introduced yet. If X is a member of set Y, you must compare X to all OTHER members of set Y, you cannot say X is better than Y because that means that X is better than itself.
So we must say that the "movie" is better than any "other" movie of the year, otherwise we're saying that the movie is better than itself.

13) If you decide someday that she was the one for you, and that she was better than any *other* girl you had known, you run the risk that she will not be available to you at that time—that your timing will just not align.

14) Art classes in European classrooms, unlike *art classes* in American classrooms, often focus more on theory and appreciation than on actively creating art.

15) More and more, modern songwriters, like medieval composers, are opting for simplistic beats and melodies instead of overly complicated ones.
Correct as is.

16) The air-conditioning units of new, "eco-friendly" homes are much cleaner and more efficient than *those of* older homes.

17) To music writers of the time, the songs of the The Beatles were as entertaining, if not more so, than *the songs of* Elvis.

18) In the modern world, unlike the past *world*, people often communicate via the internet, and friends sometimes go long periods of time without seeing each other face-to-face.

-or-

In the modern world, unlike *that of* the past, people often communicate via the internet, and friends sometimes go long periods of time without seeing each other face-to-face. NO ERROR
Arguably, this could also be correct as is. But the modern world is a physical as well as a temporal place, whereas the past is merely a temporal place, so to be proper and specific we would want to compare the "modern world" to the "past world."

19) Even today, in many parts of the world disabled people are treated like *burdens*, or worse yet, like non-*citizens*.
This is a very specialized form of faulty comparison which usually is classified as a noun-agreement error. We must compare "people" (plural) to "burdens" (plural). A more common way to see this error tested is a sentence like, "When the girls grow up, they want to become a photographer" (correct: "When the girls grow up they want to become photographers").

20) Entertaining and throwing parties in the day is not at all like *throwing parties at* night when the natural energy levels mellow, people are more likely to imbibe, and the event naturally has an air of intrigue.

21) It is somewhat paradoxical that thriving at college is somewhat less difficult than *thriving* in high school, as one is allowed to choose one's classes and therein is allowed to have a greater sense of fulfilled intellectual curiosity.

22) The athlete had a tremendous workout—running all the stairs in the stadium—but she was warned by her coach that if she continued this overtraining she would run the risk of doing more harm *than good* to her muscle groups.

23) Among those that play chess, the aforementioned player is by far the *best.*
One can only use "better" when referring to two things. "Best" must be used when referring to three or more things, otherwise the reader wonders whom specifically is this chess player better than, and whom is he worse than?

24) Between those that play chess, the aforementioned player is by far the better.
Here "between" indicates that we're dealing with two people. When comparing two things you must use "better/worse" not "best/worst" because if A is better than B, then obviously A is the best between A and B.

25) Among my two brothers and I, my brother Ken is the obviously *best* cook.

26) Among the flautists, there are distinctions for first, and second-chair, and obviously the first-chair flautist is the best.
NO ERROR

27) I began reading the essay expecting the usual dribble so common among middle-schoolers, but by the end I was very pleasantly surprised, and I would even say that it was the *best* composition by someone of that age that I have ever seen.
You could argue that this is a stylistic error, but technically "most perfect" is redundant and the fact that the author is comparing the essay to all other essays of someone of that age, makes it a comparison, so it could be considered a faulty comparison.

28) Baseball statisticians are well-known and well-paid for tracking all the metrics of baseball players and for reporting back to management if, for example, one player scores more points than *he did in* the last game.

29) I'm eighty-six next month while my wife is only seventy-nine, so I'm thinking that statistically she has more time to live than *I*.
Arguably this is a pronoun case error, but it's also a comparison, so it goes well in this section. "Me" needs to be "I". When making comparisons, you must end the comparison in the subject-pronoun because the implication is, "more time than I (have to live)." Whereas if you end the comparison with "me" the same implication cannot be made "more time than me (has to live?)."
This is true for all comparisons that end in a pronoun: "he is taller than I" (correct) "he is taller than me" (incorrect). It gets ambiguous when you say something like "he likes bowling more than me/I" (both are correct: either he likes bowling more than he likes me, or he likes bowling more than I like bowling. But this is not the case here. There is no way that "she has more time to live than 'me'."

30) I am less hungry than *I was* an hour ago, but I'm sure I'll get an appetite once we sit down to eat.

31) The analyst had a successful half-year review, and with his new salary, he was on target to earn more than *he earned* last year.

32) At times, one has to wonder why people chose to inhabit Australia: started as a penal colony of the British, it is now home to a species of jellyfish whose venom is the only thing more poisonous than *the venom from* a bite by one of their legendary spiders.

33) Unlike those cheesy motivational posters, I would not advise you to simply "Do what you're passionate about" as you must do what is necessary, good, and lucrative, and this may not always tie in to what you're passionate about. NO ERROR

34) Similar to *where you found* your relationship, an online dating site was where I found my current girlfriend.

-or-

Similar to *you and your relationship*, I found my current girlfriend on an online dating site.
This could also be a misplaced modifier error, but it is a faulty comparison in that "your relationship" is being compared to "an online dating site."

35) In areas of strength, as in *areas of* weakness, it is important to have perspective and realize that you are not the worst, nor the best, just another one trying to excel, fighting your own battles.

36) I encourage everyone to enjoy the ride, as we cannot be sure if any moment will be better than the last or worse than the prior. NO ERROR

37) When the FBI caught the man who had been hacking into the accounts of celebrities, he commented that it was interesting how all celebrities seemed to date one another, preferring perpetual change to *stability*.

-or-

When the FBI caught the man who had been hacking into the accounts of celebrities, he commented that it was interesting how all celebrities seemed to date one another, preferring perpetually changing partners to any one person.
We don't want to compare perpetual change to a person, even if colloquially we understand what is meant.

38) I was singularly unimpressed by the nominees this year, and found no one to be better than any of the *other* nominees.

39) Earning one's fortune is far preferable to *winning the lottery*, as the former will provide you with a linear sense of success, while the latter will be like an explosion in your life.
This is almost a parallelism error, but we're comparing "earning" to "the lottery victory" so it would be better to compare "earning" to "winning."

40) In the tired and worn-out post-test phase of the six-hour exam, the candidates agreed that this *year's test* was far more challenging than the test of last year.

CHAPTER 5

Misplaced Modifiers

The most potentially humorous of all grammar errors are misplaced modifiers. They can turn a family mealtime into an entirely different event:

Correct: *Skin glistening, making my mouth water, the Thanksgiving turkey was presented to us by my grandmother.*

Incorrect (on multiple levels):
Skin glistening, making my mouth water, my grandmother presented the Thanksgiving turkey to us.

Remember that the thing being modified needs to come right after the modifying expression.

In the first example, the modifiers (skin glistening, making my mouth water) line up nicely before what they are modifying (the Thanksgiving turkey)

In the second example, the modifiers line up before "grandmother" which then literally means grandmother's skin was glistening—hopefully not the intended meaning.

Pro Tip:

It's rare to see a sentence starting with a modifier that's not testing a misplaced modifier error. Learn to watch for these types of groupings. The SAT tends to be a sterile and matter-of-fact kind of narrative test. Modifiers, are by nature, a more florid type of writing style. Knowing this, modifiers should stick out a bit (see?).

The SAT leans toward comma splices, not modifiers. The use of modifiers usually only exists to test misplaced modifiers

Practice

Most of the sentences below contain misplaced modifiers. Circle the modifier and draw an arrow to what it should be modifying.

1) You only live once; that's the motto, baby: YOLO.
2) I only ate vegetables last night, not realizing that it would be the last meal and last opportunity for my consumption of protein until after the high-holidays.
3) He mostly likes the works of the Impressionists, not to be confused with the Cubists or the Dadaists.
4) Exhausted, but somehow not zeroed, the president grew his previously-weakened coffers for reelection.
5) Presenting the medals to the children on silver platters, the director of the organization was proud of his accomplishments.
6) The painting *Icarus*, a story of the man who tried to escape his prison by creating a wing suit bound with wax, is one of Matisse's most loved works.
7) He nearly drove the wagon train off the cliff, which was steep and perilous.
8) The dog was referred to a therapist with significant problems sitting and staying.
9) It is worth mentioning that finding a letter in a mailbox that doesn't belong to the homeowner is felonious.
10) This morning I had to run outside to shoot an elephant in my pajamas.
11) The Tate Modern in London is a spectacular place to view paintings made of non-traditional materials daily.
12) Tourists to the city of St. Petersburg would do well to visit the port where ships were made at least once.
13) You must realize that your employer only cares about you to the extent that you are value accretive.
14) Understanding basic childhood development, the professor realized that children who laugh rarely are shy.

15) Themselves capable of growing to heights of hundreds of feet, sequoia is one of about seven words in the English language that uses one of each vowel; others include, eulogia and eutopia.

16) Itself an anomaly to those paying, attention was not paid by the viewers to the rock star they claimed to love so much.

17) In order to receive a high score, test anxiety must be mastered.

18) Having made the purchase at the nursery, we were informed that watering it often, the plant should not die until at least a year after purchase.

19) The Asian languages are difficult to ascertain for those who were not brought up there, but learning it well, the alphabet will serve as a linchpin of one's future reading and writing endeavors.

20) Heady with hedonism, filled with fillings, stymied by steam, the boiling water on the stove deterred the passionate dental patient from finishing the preparation of dinner.

21) I realized, too late, but were that it would have been too soon, that having half the plot depth and none of the character development, I was writing a novel that would never hold up to my publisher's requirements.

22) You lament your lack of weight loss from abiding by the stringent rules of the strange diet, but my question to you is, was the diet even weight loss?

23) Yesterday, I saw a horse and a cow passing by a field on the way to the portrait studio.

24) Having gained fame from her roles in major motion pictures, true die-hard fans will remember that the actress actually received her SAG card from having been in an episode of reality TV.

25) The lone survivors were discovered dehydrated and scorched by the coast guard.

26) The crime, horse theft, was committed in front of two police officers while they were standing and sleeping, as they are known to do.

27) He was internationally acclaimed and eventually won the Nobel Peace Prize for his works that ended up yielding to him quite a bit of money.

28) Climbers of Everest, or even those who intend merely the ascent to base camp, are told to throw away excess materials and to cleanse their minds, if they have any.

29) Take it seriously but don't overemphasize it: these things that we think of as important now, tied down by the trappings of other people's ideas of success, are not necessarily what we will find important in ten, or even five, years.

30) Come graduation day you will receive lucrative envelopes and sage pieces of advice worth more than the contents and all the envelopes, which you are encouraged to store in the recesses of your mind.

31) It's a fairly cushy gig: stay up and watch the dogs pace if you need something to keep you alert during the long nights.

32) Effectively ending his racing career, the man was struck by the strangeness of the situation in watching a horse who had spent his whole life racing succumb to a condition as non-threatening as gout, caused by the jockey giving him too much rich food.

33) Men who gamble frequently are reminded of the duality of their addictions: only losing gamblers have a problem, while winning ones are lucky.

34) The reason we mark-to-market our accounts so often is to decrease the rampant credit risk of holding unhedged positions.

35) Becoming a grand-master, the openings of chess, the gambits, and the point-value of pieces must be mastered.

36) Having had the faith that he had had, the minister was undaunted by the fact that, halved, his church attendance was reduced.

37) He showed me the sentence, "let's eat grandma" and, "let's eat, grandma" and dared me to again insist, as I had previously, those commas that are used frequently are misused.

38) Personified by the anthropomorphic nature of poetry, I was transported by the animals in the works of Ogden Nash, who so adroitly captures their folly and misadventures in his poems.

39) Don't be surprised if, when asked about their financial status—wages, taxes, charitable contributions—many people's first reaction is silence.

40) *The Planets*, light-years away and celestial by nature, is one of Holst's greatest works, and one that is named after the heavens.

Answers

1) You live only once; that's the motto, baby: YOLO.
Courtesy of Lil' Wayne and Drake, this is a misplaced modifier as "only" is modifying "live" (i.e., you merely live) when it should be modifying "once" (i.e., you live only one time).

2) I ate only vegetables last night, not realizing that it would be the last meal and last opportunity for my consumption of protein until after the high-holidays.
Similar to the one above, the emphasis is on the fact that no meat was consumed, so the proper placement of "only" is before "vegetables" suggesting that was the only thing consumed, not that the author merely ate.

3) He mostly likes the works of the Impressionists, not to be confused with the Cubists or the Dadaists. NO ERROR
"mostly" is an adverb and it doesn't matter if it comes before or after likes because it cannot modify anything other than "likes." If we wanted to say that he liked "most of the works of the impressionists" then we would need the adjective "most"

4) Exhausted, but somehow not zeroed, the president's previously-weakened coffers were grown for reelection.
This is very tricky, but once you weed through the comma splices, you see that the subject of the sentence is the president's coffers, not the president. So we need to place "coffers" right after the modifier "somehow not zeroed." Also, a person cannot be zeroed, but resources can.
The cleanest way to convert this to an appropriate sentence also involves turning it into a passive-voice sentence "coffers were grown" which is sub-optimal, but we're not testing active/passive voice here, in this specific section. If you ran into this on the SAT, there would be a reworded version such that you could keep the sentence in the active voice.

5) Presenting the medals on silver platters to the children, the director of the organization was proud of his accomplishments.
Medals are on platters, not the children.

6) The painting shares its title with the myth of Icarus, a story of the man who tried to escape his prison by creating a wing suit bound with wax, and is one of Matisse's most loved works.
This is very tricky but the painting is not a story, so you cannot modify the painting with "a story." The painting shares its title with the story, so you can rephrase the sentence to indicate this however you like, but it is incorrect as is.

7) He drove the wagon train nearly off the cliff, which was steep and perilous.
Again we deal with single word modifiers. The intent is most likely that the man drove the wagon train "nearly" off the cliff, not that he "nearly drove" which is difficult to conceptualize.

8) The dog with significant problems sitting and staying was referred to a therapist.
Here is a modifier not set-off by a comma. Still, it is likely that the therapist was not the one with sitting and staying problems, and thus as stated, the sentence is incorrect.

9) It is worth mentioning that finding a letter that doesn't belong to the homeowner, in a mailbox is felonious. *It is impossible for a mailbox to not belong to the homeowner.*

10) This morning I had to run outside in my pajamas to shoot an elephant.

11) The Tate Modern in London is a spectacular place to view daily paintings made of non-traditional materials.

12) Tourists to the city of St. Petersburg would do well to visit, at least once, the port where ships were made.

13) You must realize that your employer cares about you only to the extent that you are value accretive.

14) Understanding basic childhood development, the professor realized that children who rarely laugh are shy */or/* children who laugh are rarely shy.

15) The tree capable of growing to heights of hundreds of feet, sequoia is one of seven words in the English language that uses one of each vowel; others include, eulogia and eutopia.

16) Anomalistically to those paying, attention was not paid by the viewers to the rock star they claimed to love so much.

17) In order to receive a high score, you must master test anxiety.

18) Having made the purchase at the nursery, we were informed that watered often, the plant should not die until at least a year after purchase.
We have to delete "it" otherwise the suggestion is that the plant would water itself.

19) The Asian languages are difficult to ascertain for those who were not brought up there, but learned well, the alphabet will serve as a linchpin of one's future reading and writing endeavors.
Similar explanation to the one above.

20) Heady with hedonism, filled with fillings, stymied by steam, the dentist was deterred by the boiling water on the stove from hitting on the patient.

21) I realized, too late, but were that it would have been too soon, that having half the plot depth and none of the character development, the novel I was writing would never hold up to my publisher's requirements.

22) You lament your lack of weight loss from abiding by the stringent rules of the strange diet, but my question to you is, was the diet designed for weight loss?

23) Yesterday, passing by a field on the way to the portrait studio, I saw a horse and a cow.

24) Having gained fame from her roles in major motion pictures, the actress actually received her SAG card from having been in an episode of reality TV, as true die-hard fans will remember.

25) The coast guard discovered dehydrated and scorched survivors.

26) The crime, horse theft, was committed in front of two police officers while the officers –or-- while the horses were standing and sleeping, as they are known to do.

27) He was internationally acclaimed and eventually won the Nobel Peace Prize, which ended up yielding to him quite a bit of money, for his work.

28) Climbers of Everest, or even those who intend merely the ascent to base camp, are told to throw away excess materials, if they have any, and to cleanse their minds.

29) Take it seriously but don't overemphasize it: these things that we, tied down by the trappings of other people's ideas of success, think of are not necessarily what we will find important in ten, or even five, years.

30) Come graduation day you will receive lucrative envelopes and sage pieces of advice, which you are encouraged to store in the recesses of your mind, worth more than the contents and all the envelopes.

31) It's a fairly cushy gig: stay up and watch the dogs; pace if you need something to keep you alert during the long nights.

32) Effectively ending the horse's career, the man was struck by the strangeness of the situation in watching a horse who had spent his whole life racing succumb to a condition as non-threatening as gout, caused by the jockey giving him too much rich food.

33) Men who frequently gamble are/who gamble are frequently reminded of the duality of their addictions: only losing gamblers have a problem, while winning ones are lucky.

34) The reason we so often mark-to-market our accounts is to decrease the rampant credit risk of holding unhedged positions.

35) To become a grand master, the openings of chess, the gambits, and the point-value of pieces must be mastered.

36) Having had the faith that he had had, the minister was undaunted by the fact that, halved, his church's attendance was reduced.

37) He showed me the sentence, "let's eat grandma" and, "let's eat, grandma" and dared me to again insist, as I had previously, those commas that are frequently used are misused.

38) Personified by the anthropomorphic nature of poetry, the animals in the works of Ogden Nash, who so adroitly captures their folly and misadventures in his poems, transported me.

39) Don't be surprised if, when asked about their financial status—wages, taxes, charitable contributions—many people react with silence at first.

40) One of Holst's greatest works, and one that is named after the heavens, light-years away and celestial by nature, is The Planets. NOTE: The Planets is the name of a symphony, and does not refer to the actual planets.

CHAPTER 6

Noun Agreement

This is certainly one of the more challenging errors that the SAT tests. Just as pronoun/antecedent errors require you to identify the antecedent that each pronoun refers to, so too do noun agreement questions require you to find exactly what noun another noun refers to.

The one factor you have in your favor is that there are not very many things that can be wrong with a solitary noun, so if one is underlined, or in question, there is only one question to ask: does it agree in quantity with its antecedent?

Example:

Incorrect: *The girls want to become a photographer*

Correct: *The girls want to become photographers*

There are no great tips for conquering this error type, and the best thing you can do to prepare yourself is simply expose yourself to a large number of sentences that abuse this error.

Practice

Most of the following sentences contain noun-agreement errors. Circle the errant noun and indicate whether it needs to be changed to singular or plural.

1) The fringe groups need to immediately come to the center and show solidarity or the rest of the country will risk being labeled traitors.

2) Whereas I may be convinced of your plan, the rest of the family will remain intransigent and would prefer to be a dissenter than to capitulate to what you're suggesting.

3) This sales spread was previously predicted to compress, but now as it expands, it has implications for rent and NOI, which usually follow directionally and with a larger amplitude.

4) After a recession, economists usually expect GDP to continue upward followed by a healthy consumer price index and new job creation both of which usually tend to serve as a lagging indicator.

5) At completion, and if successful, the board, which includes Jeffersons serving as Managing Trustee and President, will be replaced by five new trustees.

6) The leader of the association will pin a medal on the co-captains to commemorate their service to their team.

7) The coach told the team that each had to be team players in order for the team to succeed.

8) In order for the effort to succeed, the ensemble needed to become a unit, and the members needed to be synchronous.

9) Each of the twins was kind and respectful, deferent to her elders and conscientious of her community, so the fact that they decided to become a philanthropist upon graduating college came as a surprise to no one.

10) The couple was inseparable, and their love was an old one, as they had known each other since they were a child.

11) To assume that your countrymen deserve to be victorious in their war is asinine: has there ever been a nation whose warriors, all as brave as those who came before them and as brave as those who will come after, did not desire to be a conquering, all-consuming winner?

12) The union members and the union itself are valiant constituents in a fight against the tyranny of oppression.

13) They look at the works of Pollock and Twombly claiming that the works are a bore, not realizing that these are and were the forerunners of modern art.

14) These films are riveting and their plot thoroughly engrossing.

15) Because the casseroles turned out to be a congealed and bland mess, we opted to go out to dinner, which turned out not much better.

16) There are certain franchises, those which serve freshly baked donuts and coffee, and those which will freshly prepare a hamburger at any time of the night, which I see in my mind as a shining bastion of American hospitality.

17) Before boarding the plane, a passenger must present tickets to the boarding agent, who will scan it, confirm that the seat is available, and bid the passenger a pleasant flight.

18) The parents bade their daughters a pleasant trip, and the girls would need it, as one was on her way to Europe via shipping barge, and the other was going to Peru via the Panama Canal.

19) The office spaces, catty-corner from the fabric resellers and the still-more blighted warehouses, have become an eyesore that the community has rightly elected to rid itself of.

20) Remember when the parks were the crown-jewel of the city, and try to get us back to a place where that can be true once more.

21) The brains of an infant are not as well developed as those of their older counterparts; namely it is lacking the ability to process complex thoughts and second-order interrogatives.

22) All soccer players want to score a goal: it is in their DNA.

23) Imagine the reality-show contestant's disappointment when the host told him that his prized violins were in fact forged and were collectively worth no more than a base-model cello.

24) The convention attendees gave a warm welcome to the very motivational speaker who had, the year before, labeled them grave disappointments to the cause.

25) The idea of a parent teacher conference for a preschooler is somewhat overstated as one does not take too seriously a teachers comment that their son or daughter has developed a refined abilities for the skills of cutting and pasting.

26) The Olympic coaches used to argue over the girls, for they possessed unique talents for both bobsledding and skiing, but, due to logistical conflicts, could not compete in both events.

27) After their first date, the man texted the woman something witty about a shared interest, to which she bantered and replied that she loved men who take the initiative.

28) My four daughters will grow up to be either senators, doctors, or lawyers, thanks to the fortunes bestowed upon us by our faithful clientele.

29) Don't forget stories like *The Boy Who Cried Wolf* and *The Tortoise and The Hare* which serve as a sharp admonishments to he who underestimates the gravity of situations.

30) The unions and the members of the unions demanded, among nearly everything else, a healthcare plan that would grant 17-weeks of paternity leave.

31) The need of the community is not the same as the needs of the members who want for access to healthcare and clean water.

32) His superiors granted him the promotion he requested, recognizing in him a strong abilities for problem solving and client interactions.

33) Last night it seems we both had the thought that additional subsidies would do more to harm than help the young country.

34) I give you the countries of Zimbabwe and Malawi as an examples of places where the average life expectancy is decreasing.

35) If you allow that Picasso was a precursor of Rothko then you must simultaneously allow that Monet and Cezanne were precursors of Serat.

36) Species of birds are as varied as grains of sand on the beach, but their needs differ little.

37) The reasons for the horses' odd behavior is not hard to interpolate: clearly they are underfed and overexposed to the elements.

38) The reasons for the horse's odd behavior is not hard to interpolate: clearly it is underfed and overexposed to the elements.

39) The reason for the horse's odd behavior is not hard to interpolate: clearly it is a combination of being underfed and overexposed to the elements.

40) I misunderstood the questions' purposes which were to illustrate the intelligence of the asker, not condemn the stupidity of the answerer.

Answers

1) The fringe groups need to immediately come to the center and show solidarity or the rest of the country will risk being *labeled a traitor*.

2) Whereas I may be convinced of your plan, the rest of the family will remain intransigent and would prefer to *be dissenters* than to capitulate to what you're suggesting.

3) This sales spread was previously predicted to compress, but now as it expands, it has implications for rent and NOI, which usually follow directionally and with *larger amplitudes*.

4) After a recession, economists usually expect GDP to continue upward followed by a healthy consumer price index and new job creation both of which usually tend to serve as *lagging indicators*.

5) At completion, and if successful, the board, which includes Jeffersons serving as Managing Trustee and President, will be replaced by five new trustees. NO ERROR

6) The leader of the association will pin *medals* on the co-captains to commemorate their service to their team.

7) The coach told the team that each had to be *a team player* in order for the team to succeed.

8) In order for the effort to succeed, the ensemble needed to become a unit, and the members needed to be synchronous. NO ERROR

9) Each of the twins was kind and respectful, deferent to her elders and conscientious of her community, so the fact that they decided to become *philanthropists* upon graduating college came as a surprise to no one.

10) The couple was inseparable, and their love was an old one, as they had known each other since they were *children*.

11) To assume that your countrymen deserve to be victorious in their war is asinine: has there ever been a nation whose warriors, all as brave as those who came before them and as brave as those who will come after, did not desire to be ~~a~~ conquering, all-consuming *winners*?

12) The union members and the union itself are valiant constituents in a fight against the tyranny of oppression. NO ERROR

13) They look at the works of Pollock and Twombly claiming that the works are *bores*, not realizing that these are and were the forerunners of modern art.

14) These films are riveting and their *plots* thoroughly engrossing.

15) Because the casseroles turned out to be ~~a~~ congealed and bland *messes*, we opted to go out to dinner, which turned out not much better.

16) There are certain franchises, those which serve freshly baked donuts and coffee, and those which will freshly prepare a hamburger at any time of the night, which I see in my mind as ~~a~~ shining *bastions* of American hospitality.

17) Before boarding the plane, a passenger must present *a ticket* to the boarding agent, who will scan it, confirm that the seat is available, and bid the passenger a pleasant flight.

18) The parents bade their daughters *pleasant trips*, and the girls would need it, as one was on her way to Europe via shipping barge, and the other was going to Peru via the Panama Canal.

19) The office spaces, catty-corner from the fabric resellers and the still-more blighted warehouses, have become *eyesores* that the community has rightly elected to rid itself of.

20) Remember when the parks were the crown-*jewels* of the city, and try to get us back to a place where that can be true once more.

21) The brains of ~~an~~ *infants* are not as well developed as those of their older counterparts; namely *they are* lacking the ability to process complex thoughts and second-order interrogatives.

22) All soccer players want to score a *goals*: it is in their DNA.

23) Imagine the reality-show contestant's disappointment when the host told him that his prized violins were in fact forged and were collectively worth no more than a base-model cello. NO ERROR

24) The convention attendees gave a warm welcome to the very motivational speaker who had, the year before, labeled them grave *disappointments* to the cause.

25) The idea of a parent teacher conference for a preschooler is somewhat overstated as one does not take too seriously a teachers comment that their son or daughter has developed ~~a~~ refined *abilities* for the skills of cutting and pasting.

26) The Olympic coaches used to argue over the girls, for they possessed unique *talents* for both bobsledding and skiing, but, due to logistical conflicts, could not compete in both events.

27) After their first date, the man texted the woman something witty about a shared interest, to which she bantered and replied that she loved men who take the *initiatives.*

28) My four daughters will grow up to be *either senators, doctors, or lawyers,* thanks to the fortunes bestowed upon us by our faithful clientele.

29) Don't forget stories like *The Boy Who Cried Wolf* and *The Tortoise and The Hare* which serve as ~~a~~ sharp *admonishments* to he who underestimates the gravity of situations.

30) The unions and the members of the unions demanded, among nearly everything else, a healthcare plan that would grant 17-weeks of paternity leave. NO ERROR

31) The need of the community is not the same as the *needs* of the members who want for access to healthcare and clean water.

32) His superiors granted him the promotion he requested, recognizing in him ~~a~~ strong *abilities* for problem solving and client interactions.

33) Last night it seems we both had the thought that additional subsidies would do more to harm than help the young country. NO ERROR

34) I give you the countries of Zimbabwe and Malawi as ~~an~~ *examples* of places where the average life expectancy is decreasing.

35) If you allow that Picasso was a precursor of Rothko then you must simultaneously allow that Monet and Cezanne were *precursors* of Serat.

36) Species of birds are as varied as grains of sand on the beach, but their needs differ little. NO ERROR

37) The *reasons* for the horses' odd behavior is not hard to interpolate: clearly they are underfed and overexposed to the elements.

38) The *reasons* for the horse's odd behavior is not hard to interpolate: clearly it is underfed and overexposed to the elements.

39) The reason for the horse's odd behavior is not hard to interpolate: clearly it is a combination of being underfed and overexposed to the elements. NO ERROR

40) I misunderstood the questions' *purposes* which *were* to illustrate the intelligence of the asker, not condemn the stupidity of the answerer.

CHAPTER 7

Parallelism

Parallelism errors are hard to spot but easy to correct. The reason parallelism is challenging is because it can be violated both within a single clause and between multiple clauses.

Within-clause errors:

Incorrect: *I like to run, to jump, and sleeping.*

Correct: *I like to run, to jump, and to sleep.*

Multiple-clause errors:

Incorrect: *To suggest that advertising dollars are ill-spent is asserting that consumers are not malleable.*

Correct: *To suggest that advertising dollars are ill-spent is to assert that consumers are not malleable.*

The first one is far easier to spot: when an author lists attributes, be sure they are all the same parts of speech and presented congruently.

The second one is more of a challenge and requires that you track your verbs. Keep note of what form your first verb comes in so that you can see if your second one matches.

Practice

Most of the following sentences contain parallelism errors. Correct them where you find them.

1) To argue that the resilient nature of certain bacteria to current antibiotics is a reason to cease the prescription of all antibiotics is like arguing that because some cars do not have airbags no one should drive.

2) Allow me to argue the point that to cull and select between two things is the height of being human, and in fact it is identical to the process used in identifying and evaluating all options.

3) It is well done and sturdy in construction, but that will not be enough to ensure its seaworthiness should storms come in.

4) For a job done well and on time, you can do no better than to call my handy man who brings his own tools, purchases his own materials, and always leaves the site clean.

5) In preparing a fantasy football team, one would do well to choose one player for kicking, one player who has a strong history of non-safety returns greater than 30 yards, and at least three linebackers who are of at least 300 lbs.

6) The Olympic uniforms were hailed by designers, but frustrated fans who thought the Olympics should contain an element of egalitarianism and an air of homogeneity.

7) A steak done well is a steak well done and finished with a pinch of sea salt.

8) My mother, a chef who is seasoned in seasonings, is someone who likes cooking, and to while away an afternoon reading is not something that would be out of the realm of imagination.

9) My mother, a chef who is seasoned in seasonings, is someone who likes cooking and to while away an afternoon reading something that would be out of the realm of imagination.

10) There were two meals a day for the warriors who ate voraciously in the morning and noon.

11) Are you truly interested in helping people concerned with the recent flooding, or are you merely seeking another vignette to post on your resume?

12) Are you truly interested in helping people, concerned with the recent flooding, or are you merely seeking another vignette to post on your resume?

13) A precocious youth, Anne Boleyn was one bothered, anxious, and worried about the increasing disparity in wealth that people in her country faced.

14) I cannot seem to figure out what the candidate stands for other than it seems like he is for winning and not losing.

15) The novelist has a following of women who seem to despise happiness and loathe being content—a group who singularly seems to evoke emotions of both sympathy and empathy while simultaneously projecting repugnancy.

16) He expects that he will not only receive a gold medal from the half pipe competition, obtain praise via the international community, but perform a perfect 1440 off the ski jump—a most unusual feat.

17) As an academician, I find the professor not only intelligent but also pleasant to work with.

18) His daughter was his favorite child: blonde, wise, and well read, she had all the characteristics that he himself had wanted to engender.

19) Prisoners seem to be perpetually pursuing increased levels of freedom without realizing the irony of their situation: either they must obey the rules of society and avail themselves to all the freedoms that life has to offer, or be incarcerated.

20) When volunteering for service in their country, one either must join the army, the navy, or the marines.

21) They are neither our friends nor are they our enemies, as they merely occupy a middle-ground somewhere between the end of the world and the beginning of space.

22) An old proverb goes something like, "all the world is a very narrow bridge, but the important thing is not to be afraid at all" and I take this to mean that we need not be either terrified nor should we be dismissive of the difficulties that come to us.

23) I am in the house but not hungry.

24) I am in the house but not Hungary.

25) She wasn't happy before, but I made her so, and I can make you as well.

26) A chef's job is multifaceted: he must endeavor to please his guests and their stomachs but not upset the pocketbooks of anyone.

27) This smoothie she makes daily is disgusting, and it makes it seem like she wants to live forever, to keep the kale market bubbling, and like she wants to impart this lifestyle on others.

28) The council must have patience with the girls, realizing that learning the system as an adult is much harder than to try to learn the system as a child.

29) Jon is happy and forty-two years old.

30) Jonathan accused John of slander in the office on Monday, and of libel on Wednesday.

31) I was fortified by the fruits of the land, made strong by the slings of my opponents, calloused by their comments, and so can you.

32) After the analyst took his Series 7 exam—a 7 hour test—he was tired, was thirsty, and fearful that his score was not high enough.

33) After the analyst took his Series 7 exam—a 7 hour test—he was tired, thirsty, and was fearful that his score was not high enough.

34) After the analyst took his Series 7 exam—a 7 hour test—he was tired and thirsty, and was fearful that his score was not high enough.

35) You need not be fearful of the consequences, but you need to be cognizant of the gravity of the situation.

36) The property manager owned nearly 10,000 square feet of property which was rapidly appreciating on the heels of increasing Net Operating Income numbers which were themselves boosted by increased cap rates.

37) They who clean our room should not be relegated to an out-property, but instead let us welcome them into our homes with the warmth they deserve.

38) The depth of the so called Deep Web is deeply unsettling, telling us that the millions of webpages and billions of terabytes of data are not indexed by crawlers and shuttle and show illicit content.

39) In forgotten depths of darkness lie the places angels deign to fly, and in those depths where loss is found, a deafening din is said to sound like retreating fervor on love's last ground, and those who fight won't last the night, but still insist their cause is right, honorable, and worth the plight.

40) It might be uncouth to like a corporately-produced product this much, but I love the taste of iced coffee that is made just for me.

Answers

1) To argue that the resilient nature of certain bacteria to current antibiotics is a reason to cease the prescription of all antibiotics *IS TO ARGUE* that because some cars do not have airbags no one should drive.

2) Allow me to argue the point that to cull and select between two things is the height of being human, and in fact it is identical to the process used *TO IDENTIFY AND EVALUATE* all options.

3) It is *WELL DONE AND STURDILY BUILT / GOOD AND STURDY*, but that will not be enough to ensure its seaworthiness should storms come in.
We must use two adverbs (well done and sturdily) or we can use two adjectives (good and sturdy)

4) For a job done *WELL AND TIMELY*, you can do no better than to call my handy man who brings his own tools, purchases his own materials, and always leaves the site clean.
Again we must keep the parallelism of the form of the descriptors and use two adverbs.

5) In preparing a fantasy football team, one would do well to choose *ONE PLAYER WHO KICKS*, one player who has a strong history of non-safety returns greater than 30 yards, and at least three linebackers who are of at least 300 lbs.

6) The Olympic uniforms were hailed by designers, *BUT WERE FRUSTRATING TO* fans who thought the Olympics should contain an element of egalitarianism and an air of homogeneity.

7) A steak done well is a steak well done and finished with a pinch of sea salt. NO ERROR

8) My mother, a chef who is seasoned in seasonings, is someone who likes cooking, and to while away an afternoon reading is not something that would be out of the realm of imagination. NO ERROR

9) My mother, a chef who is seasoned in seasonings, is someone who likes cooking and *WHILING* away an afternoon reading something that would be out of the realm of imagination.

10) There were two meals a day for the warriors who ate voraciously in the morning *AND AT* noon.

11) Are you truly interested in helping people concerned with the recent flooding, or are you merely seeking another vignette to post on your resume? NO ERROR

12) Are you truly interested in helping people, *CONCERNED BY* the recent flooding, or are you merely seeking another vignette to post on your resume?

13) A precocious youth, Anne Boleyn was one *BOTHERED BY*, anxious, and worried about the increasing disparity in wealth that people in her country faced.

14) I cannot seem to figure out what the candidate stands for other than it seem like he is for winning and *NOT FOR LOSING*.

15) The novelist has a following of women who seem to despise happiness and *LOATHE CONTENTEDNESS* —a group who singularly seems to evoke emotions of both sympathy and empathy while simultaneously projecting repugnancy.

16) He expects that he will not only receive a gold medal from the half pipe competition, obtain praise via the international community, *BUT ALSO* perform a perfect 1440 off the ski jump—a most unusual feat.

17) As an academician, I find the professor not only intelligent but also pleasant. *OMIT "to work with"*
"The professor" is *adjective* and *adjective. We don't want to say, "the professor"* is *adjective* and *subordinate clause.*

18) His daughter was his favorite child: blonde, wise, and *SCHOLARLY/BOOK SMART*, she had all the characteristics that he himself had wanted to engender.
"Well read" is an adverb; we need to keep the list: adjectives only.

19) Prisoners seem to be perpetually pursuing increased levels of freedom without realizing the irony of their situation: *THEY MUST EITHER OBEY* the rules of society, and avail themselves to all the freedoms that life has to offer, or *THEY MUST STAY IN PRISON*.

There are a few errors nested here. First, the misplaced modifier: the "either" is placed in the wrong spot. Second, the original sentence also violates parallelism by saying "they must....or." It's preferable to say "they must x or they must y." Finally, "they must obey" is active, while "be incarcerated" is passive. Change both to agree in voice.

20) When volunteering for service in their country, *ONE MUST JOIN EITHER* the army, the navy, or the marines. *Similar to the error above: a misplaced modifier makes this parallelism hard to spot.*

21) They are neither our friends *NOR OUR ENEMIES*, as they merely occupy a middle-ground somewhere between the end of the world and the beginning of space.
We can either say, "they are neither our friends, but they are not our enemies either" to keep the "they are" parallelism, but that is a bit wordy. So instead we'll say "they are neither x nor y."

22) An old proverb goes something like, "all the world is a very narrow bridge, but the important thing is not to be afraid at all" and I take this to mean that we need not be ~~either~~ terrified nor ~~should we be~~ dismissive of the difficulties that come to us. OMIT

23) I am in the house but not hungry. NO ERROR

24) I am in the house but not Hungary. NO ERROR
The person is in one of his many houses and is specifying that he is not in the home in the country of Hungary.

25) She wasn't happy before, but I made her so, and I can make *YOU HAPPY* as well.

26) A chef's job is multifaceted: he must endeavor to please his guests and their stomachs but *NOT UPSET ANYONE'S POCKETBOOK.*

27) This smoothie she makes daily is disgusting, and it makes it seems like she wants to live forever, to keep the kale market bubbling, and ~~like she wants~~ to impart this lifestyle on others. OMIT

28) The council must have patience with the girls, realizing that learning the system as an adult is much harder than *TRYING TO LEARN* the system as a child.

29) Jon is happy and forty-two years old. NO ERROR

30) Jonathan accused John of slander in the office on Monday, and of libel on Wednesday. NO ERROR

31) I was fortified by the fruits of the land, made strong by the slings of my opponents, calloused by their comments, and so can you. NO ERROR
There is an implied, "so can you be made so" so there is no error.

32) After the analyst took his Series 7 exam—a 7 hour test—he was tired, was thirsty, and *WAS* fearful that his score was not high enough.

33) After the analyst took his Series 7 exam—a 7 hour test—he was tired, *WAS* thirsty, and was fearful that his score was not high enough.

34) After the analyst took his Series 7 exam—a 7 hour test—he was tired and thirsty, and was fearful that his score was not high enough. NO ERROR
But it could also be revised, "and fearful that"

35) You need not be fearful of the consequences, but you need ~~TO~~ be cognizant of the gravity of the situation. OMIT *The first clause is in the form of the naked infinitive so we need to revise the second clause to the same.*

36) The property manager owned nearly 10,000 square feet of property which was rapidly appreciating on the heels of increasing Net Operating Income numbers which were themselves *BEING BOOSTED BY OR BOOSTED BY* increasing cap rates.

37) They who clean our room should not be relegated to an out-property, but *BE WELCOMED* into our homes with the warmth they deserve.

38) The depth of the so called *Deep Web* is deeply unsettling, telling us that *CRAWLERS DO NOT INDEX MILLIONS OF WEBPAGES AND BILLIONS OF TERABYTES OF DATA THAT SHUTTLE AND SHOW* illicit content.
We want to avoid switching voices here.

39) In forgotten depths of darkness lie the places angels deign to fly, and in those depths where loss is found, a deafening din is said to sound like retreating fervor on love's last ground, and those who fight won't last the night, but still insist their cause is right, honorable, and *WORTHY*.
There are any number of ways to change this. It doesn't matter what you choose, just realize that "worth the plight" is incongruous with "right, honorable"

40) It might be uncouth to like a corporately-produced product this much, but I love the taste of Starbucks iced coffee *THAT BARISTAS MAKE FOR ME.*
There's a voice shift in "love"(active) to "is made"(passive). Change them to match.

CHAPTER 8

Prepositions

Possibly the most frustrating of all English conventions, prepositions follow absolutely no rules, standards, or patterns.

There is no reason we say:

I am studying the history of *Russia* instead of *I am studying the history* about *Russia*.

And the only way we know one is better than the other, is by ear.

Yes, there are lists which spell out which preposition every single verb takes (excited *for*, in love *with*, dreaming *about*) but to memorize these would be a huge misallocation of time.

Do as many problems as you can get your hands on, and start noticing which prepositions make sense and which don't. Sometimes, noting the oddity of a thing will help you remember.

Does it make any sense why you would be *angry* with *someone*, but *mad* at them?

Pro Tip

These are very hard errors to correct, so usually the SAT tests them with approximately the same frequency, in approximately the same section, and usually calls attention to the error. In the current version of the SAT (pre March 2016) the SAT tests (almost always) 2 preposition errors per test, between numbers 22 and 28 on the 35-question writing section. Look for this predictability to persist on the New SAT.

Practice

Most sentences contain a misused preposition. Identify it and write the correct one. Sometimes the correct answer will be to delete the preposition instead of replacing.

1) Inside of the cave, behind the tree, and below the small slit of light that filtered down through the musty air, there lay a bear.

2) Next time you are in the South of France, promise me you shall call me up and that we will enjoy an afternoon together.

3) Do not let us jump in the lake until after we have thoroughly applied a layer of SPF 100 sunscreen over all our exposed skin.

4) We see an often cartoonish threat of an angry woman hitting her husband over the head with a frying pan.

5) We are not the same; I am different than you in nearly every aspect imaginable.

6) You act decisive and headstrong, but when it comes down to it, you struggle with options like the rest of us: you can scarcely choose between flute, oboe, or clarinet.

7) Among the two girls exists a bond, not commonly found in people of their age.

8) Not to sound too similar to a micromanager, but my thought is, if one pays for a job, one should expect a certain level of control about it.

9) The diplomat was chastised for his perceived prejudices about the Dutch, but ostensibly not for his favoring the Germans.

10) The shipmates strived to gain at least a nebulous view about the shallow-bottomed harbor into which they were to navigate.

11) The chef was adamant that his pupils not clean up after themselves until they were completely through cooking, lest they lose time by going back and forth.

12) My life's primary satisfaction was derived by coding computer programs, so I decided to teach computer science.

13) For the untrained ear, the music of Glass will evoke the tired question, "that's music?" but to me, it is perfect.

14) One of the primary reasons that excessive drinking can be so costly is when drunk, the imbiber stops caring for money.

15) You do not need to pull the door after you enter, as it will close for itself.

16) In 8:00 AM, few things make sense, but after a strong cup of coffee and some yoga-lates, most feel better.

17) The marathoner was more interested in having his times go down than in relaxing in his vacation.

18) His daughter was a radical left-wing activist, so it was not surprising to us that she nearly disowned her father over his working in the CIA.

19) Football players tend to show preference toward captains on their teams who reflect respect toward their teammates.

20) You are not an octogenarian; a woman in your age does not need to be endowed with the benefits of a facelift, nor burdened by the costs of one.

21) He is enamored at the idea of being your husband: it pervades his thoughts and invades his dreams.

22) Call it what you may, but the notion of the privatization of Social Security is something I prefer tenfold over school vouchers.

23) I find myself concerned with how much the Democratic candidate is choosing to pander to the far left, while I find myself distraught over the amount to which the Republican candidate is choosing to pander to the right.

24) These issues are inherently concerned with each other: the average miles-per-gallon a car receives, and the level of restrictions on pollution which we will have to endure.

25) My father expressed to me the importance of becoming a student of the University of Pennsylvania's Wharton school, opining that its Real Estate department was renowned.

26) How can one choose veracity when revealing a truth necessarily contradicts ones values, and the withholding of information may mean the protection of disappointment?

27) The thing of the end of a movie by that director, is you never know if you are supposed to be overcome with glory or overcome by fear.

28) The senior trader admonished the junior trader that if he chose to engage in unhedged positions again, his boss almost certainly become angry at him.

29) Pollsters make a living by asking others questions, for example, "do you agree on the idea that legalization of class-1 substances would be divisive to society?"

30) Demonizing the leader from one's armchair is a path to nowhere; one must protest against the hegemony actively.

31) Students are often made to feel anxious with the large amount of tests they must take prior to graduation.

32) Ray Bradbury's novels show a preference for suspense and character development over action and instantaneous gratification.

33) We are friends, and since our families have been friends with each other for longer than either of us can remember, I have no reason to predict a terminus.

34) The lawyer's girlfriend, to whom the lawyer was soon planning on proposing marriage, was going to be in The Hamptons in the Fourth of July, and thus was preparing herself by buying a new swimsuit.

35) There is a bank located on Birch Street where it crosses Adams, and another which is too far to walk to, but is not far enough to warrant transport via a bus.

36) A strict city ordinance, not to mention the common sense employed by the populous, dictates to the masses that they are prohibited to ride bicycles on highways.

37) Divers know that an overly quick return to the surface can result in The Bends, an illness that for most is extremely detrimental for the health.

38) The circumstances were normal, but, then again, after 20 years of working the Trauma Unit of the ER, there were few things by which the doctor was alarmed.

39) All staff meetings are important, but for this one, the principal made a heartfelt plea that no teachers be absent at the congregation, for she had a special announcement.

40) The congregation were so bored by the preacher's didactic ramblings that, as if by divine intervention, a plan revealed itself unto them which allowed the congregants to cease their attendance without fear of repercussion.

Answers

1) Inside ~~of~~ the cave, behind the tree, and below the small slit of light that filtered down through the musty air, there lay a bear.

2) Next time you are in the South of France, promise me you shall call me ~~up~~ and that we will enjoy an afternoon together.

3) Do not let us jump INTO the lake until after we have thoroughly applied a layer of SPF 100 sunscreen over all our exposed skin.

4) We see an often cartoonish threat of an angry woman hitting her husband ON the head with a frying pan.

5) We are not the same; I am different FROM you in nearly every aspect imaginable.

6) You act decisive and headstrong, but when it comes down to it, you struggle with options like the rest of us: you can scarcely choose AMONG flute, oboe, or clarinet.
   "Among" is used for 3 or more things, while "between" is used for two things.

7) BETWEEN the two girls exists a bond, not commonly found in people of their age.

8) Not to sound too similar to a micromanager, but my thought is, if one pays for a job, one should expect a certain level of control OVER it.

9) The diplomat was chastised for his perceived prejudices FOR the Dutch, but ostensibly not for his favoring the Germans.

10) The shipmates strived to gain at least a nebulous view OF the shallow-bottomed harbor into which they were to navigate.

11) The chef was adamant that his pupils not clean up after themselves until they were completely through cooking, lest they lose time IN going back and forth.

12) My life's primary satisfaction was derived THROUGH coding computer programs, so I decided to teach computer science.

13) TO the untrained ear, the music of Glass will evoke the tired question, "that's music?" but to me, it is perfect.

14) One of the primary reasons that excessive drinking can be so costly is when drunk, the imbiber stops caring ABOUT money.

15) You do not need to pull the door after you enter, as it will close BY itself.

16) AT 8:00 AM, few things make sense, but after a strong cup of coffee and some yoga-lates, most feel better.

17) The marathoner was more interested in having his times go down than in relaxing DURING his vacation.

18) His daughter was a radical left-wing activist, so it was not surprising to us that she nearly disowned her father over his working FOR the CIA.

19) Football players tend to show preference toward captains OF their teams who reflect respect toward their teammates.

20) You are not an octogenarian; a woman OF your age does not need to be endowed with the benefits of a facelift, nor burdened by the costs of one.

21) He is enamored WITH the idea of being your husband: it pervades his thoughts and invades his dreams.

22) Call it what you may, but the notion of the privatization of Social Security is something I prefer tenfold TO school vouchers.

23) I find myself concerned ABOUT/BY how much the Democratic candidate is choosing to pander to the far left, while I find myself distraught over the amount to which the Republican candidate is choosing to pander to the right.

24) These issues are inherently concerned with each other: the average miles-per-gallon a car receives, and the level of restrictions on pollution which we will have to endure. NO ERROR

25) My father expressed to me the importance of becoming a student AT the University of Pennsylvania's Wharton school, opining that its Real Estate department was renowned.

26) How can one choose veracity when revealing a truth necessarily contradicts one's values, and the withholding of information may mean the protection FROM disappointment?

27) The thing ABOUT the end of a movie by that director, is you never know if you are supposed to be overcome with glory or overcome by fear.

28) The senior trader admonished the junior trader that if he chose to engage in unhedged positions again, his boss almost certainly become angry WITH him.

29) Pollsters make a living by asking others questions, for example, "do you agree WITH the idea that legalization of class-1 substances would be divisive to society?"

30) Demonizing the leader from one's armchair is a path to nowhere; one must protest ~~against~~ the hegemony actively.

31) Students are often made to feel anxious BY the large amount of tests they must take prior to graduation.

32) Ray Bradbury's novels show a preference for suspense and character development TO action and instantaneous gratification.

33) We are friends, and BECAUSE our families have been friends with each other for longer than either of us can remember, I have no reason to predict a terminus.

34) The lawyer's girlfriend, to whom the lawyer was soon planning on proposing marriage, was going to be in The Hamptons ON the Fourth of July, and thus was preparing herself by buying a new swimsuit.

35) There is a bank located AT Birch Street where it crosses Adams, and another which is too far to walk to, but is not far enough to warrant transport via a bus.

36) A strict city ordinance, not to mention the common sense employed by the populous, dictates to the masses that they are prohibited to ride bicycles on highways. NO ERROR

37) Divers know that an overly quick return to the surface can result in The Bends, an illness that for most is extremely detrimental TO the health.

38) The circumstances were normal, but, then again, after 20 years of working the Trauma Unit of the ER, there were few things AT which the doctor was alarmed.

39) All staff meetings are important, but for this one, the principal made a heartfelt plea that no teachers be absent FROM the congregation, for she had a special announcement.

40) The congregation were so bored WITH the preacher's didactic ramblings that, as if by divine intervention, a plan revealed itself unto them which allowed the congregants to cease their attendance without fear of repercussion.

CHAPTER 9

Pronoun Antecedent Agreement

Hard to spot, hard to fix, and even harder to hear, this error type is daunting. Exacerbating this is the fact that pronoun-antecedent agreement is always one of the most tested errors. This has the power to make or break your score, and no student will even approach a perfect score without mastery of this topic.

There are no tricks nor easy way to do these. You must become hyper-vigilant in identifying the antecedent of each pronoun. Once you do this, it is generally easier to see if the two agree.

Technically, pronouns must agree with their antecedents in number, person and gender.

- Number:
  - Incorrect: *The collection of books was dusty and they desperately needed to be reorganized.*
    (Pronoun: *they* is plural and antecedent: *collection* is singular)
  - Correct: *The collection of books was dusty and it desperately needed to be reorganized.*
- Person
  - Incorrect: *I don't remember if anyone left your calculator in class.*
    (Antecedent: *anyone* (third person), pronoun: *your* (second person))
  - Correct: *I don't remember if anyone left his or her calculator in class.*
- Gender
  - Incorrect: *Each member of the audience is hungry, but none will line up for food until you tell him to.*
    (Antecedent: *member* (neutral gender), pronoun: *him* (masculine gender)

- Correct: *Each member of the audience is hungry, but none will line up for food until you tell him or her to.*

Pro Tip

Though pronouns and antecedents need to agree in person, number, and gender, it's rare to see the SAT test anything other than number, so simplify your life by just asking, "are they both singular or plural?"

Remember, the following are all singular: no one, nothing, nobody, anyone, anything, anybody, someone, something, somebody, everyone, everything, everybody, one, the number, each, *and* neither.

These depend on what they are referring to, to establish whether singular or plural: none, some.

Practice

Many of the following sentences contain errant pronouns. Circle and write in the correct pronoun where errors exist.

1) The annals of history are written by winners, and as such, they dictate its content, which tends to be subjective and inherently biased.

2) A bassoonist or two oboists were needed at the concert so that each could help round out the sound of the otherwise bass heavy orchestra.

3) The patient, who was a minor, presented with orthostatic hypotension, and the attending physician was resistant to ask the family's consent to administer a pregnancy test, as the doctor could not be certain of their gender.

4) That is one of the oldest families in Europe, and though the media is constantly looking for it, they will not produce proof of rightful ownership of the realm.

5) The Alumnus proceeded to give a tremendous commencement address discussing everything from the history of the school to the quirky antics and traditions that they would propagate.

6) The administration donned their robes in preparation for the acceptance of the doctoral students' procession.

7) As a citizen of a global planet, it is important to recognize the responsibility one has to his planet, his environment, and his interpersonal cohesion.

8) The stewardess declined the businessman's invitation to come stay in his Parisian chateau, as he knew that the only real incentive was free airline miles.

9) Politics is largely an old boys' club in which a member bequeaths one's seat to his son who in turn bequeaths it to his own.

10) The Chicago Bulls are interesting in that they resemble little the docile animal on which their name is based.

11) While some say seventeen-years-old is too young to be a wedding dress fashion model, others argue that the population can effectively decide for themselves.

12) Sad songs have the seemingly ethereal quality of being able to jettison the bounds of hertz and harmonies and somehow find a reminiscence in the depths of our memories, and then peg itself to the depths of our past so that the conscious mind is forced to look back on things long since forgotten.

13) Sad music has the seemingly ethereal quality of being able to jettison the bounds of hertz and harmonies and somehow find a reminiscence in the depths of our memories, and then peg themselves to the depths of our past so that the conscious mind is forced to look back on things long since forgotten.

14) We had always known that the dictatorship was evil embodied, that it imprisoned its population, and prohibited the transmission and exchange of outside information, but to find out the depths of their misinformation campaign was truly disquieting.

15) The Olympics is an event rich with competition, athleticism, and national pride, but unfortunately, according to recent studies they do not bring the level of economic stimulation to their host countries that the committee would have the hosts believe.

16) My mom and dad have essentially presented the paragon of parenthood, as the former never wavers in understanding, counsel, or generosity, the latter is singularly grounded, offering strength and compassion in such a manner that one wonders if she is channeling saints of bygone eras.

17) If scent is the sense most strongly tied to memory, then should we not be using them to more effectively remember facts and dates, not only people and occasions?

18) The term "threepeat" was coined following the Los Angeles Lakers' third victory in which the Lakers snatched victory from their opponents using the capable talents of one Kobe Bryant.

19) The World Series is far better planned than the Super Bowl in that their games are held partially in each team's stadium, unlike the Super Bowl which is held in an arbitrary third-party's location.

20) Little of what was written, accurate as it were, proved to be useful in my researching the causes of the man's incredible memory.

21) Few of the pages written, accurate as it were, proved to be useful in my researching the causes of the man's incredible memory.

22) If another pair were to follow suit, it would be difficult for the management to be passive or not to protest their departure.

23) A trio of women approached us in the Vegas club, and although we used our best pick-up game, it would not give us phone numbers or hope of a later meet-up.

24) This is not my first rodeo, and this is not the first collection of books I have published, despite my editor's stinging criticism of their lack of character development.

25) A trio of women approached us in the Vegas club, and although we used our best pick-up game, it would not give us phone numbers or hope of a later meet-up.

26) This is not my first rodeo, and this is not the first collection of books I have published, despite my editor's stinging criticism of their lack of character development.

27) Families that dine together usually maintain their strength and cohesion long after the children move out to attend schools.

28) Either your book or your glasses will need to be moved lest I drop my book bag down and crush it.

29) I challenge you to not drop Economics as a class just because one of your classmates says they can be difficult to master.

30) My dog's favorite toys are often too dirty or too buried for his own good.

31) If you end up eating your toddler's peas and carrots, then they will probably fail to fulfill their primary purpose of child nutrition.

32) The senators' oratory did little to sway the opposing party's intransigent ideals, despite their heartfelt appeal to the children of all.

33) Christine's bull was disinclined to charge the red flags waved in front of him, and far preferred to sit under a tree and smell the flowers she would find.

34) Remember that conflicts are never clean, and that when the French invaded Russia, they ended up retreating in short order only to be plagued by the same years later.

35) The Lakers and the Spurs will never end up playing one another in the post-season, but each is twice the team that they were last season.

36) Charles, Baxter, and Sophie are Springer Spaniels with traditional haircuts, but his tail is clipped while the other two have full tails.

37) Jeff told Jim that he was a better attorney when he was attending regular meetings, and that the program has a lower recidivism rate than other forms of recovery.

38) Seth told me that Matt was impressed by his self-sufficiency, implying that military school usually had beneficial results that extended beyond the classroom.

39) Realizing that he would not be the winner, the racecar driver offered his competitor a handshake in friendship.

40) He thinks about her all the time, but insists that he made the right choice, and that in the end he will be responsible for having saved their lives, though he never expects her to see that.

41) She de-friended him on the social networks and said she'd rather not know of the intricacies of status updates, the depths of his likes and dislikes, and the new relationships it relayed back for fear that it would only hurt more acutely.

42) They tend not to like us as much since the contributions switched their directions.

Answers

1) The annals of history are written by winners, and as such, they dictate THEIR content, which tends to be subjective and inherently biased.

2) A bassoonist or two oboists were needed at the concert so that THEY could help round out the sound of the otherwise bass heavy orchestra.

3) The patient, who was a minor, presented with orthostatic hypotension, and the attending physician was resistant to ask the family's consent to administer a pregnancy test, as the doctor could not be certain of THE PATIENT'S gender.

4) That is one of the oldest families in Europe, and though the media is constantly looking for it, IT will not produce proof of rightful ownership of the realm.
   Even if this is referring to The Media, it needs to be singular.

5) The Alumnus proceeded to give a tremendous commencement address discussing everything from the history of the school to the quirky antics and traditions that IT would propagate.

6) The administration donned ITS robes in preparation for the acceptance of the doctoral students' procession.

7) As a citizen of a global planet, it is important to recognize the responsibility HE has to his planet, his environment, and his interpersonal cohesion.
   HE must agree with HIS; one is neutral.

8) The stewardess declined the businessman's invitation to come stay in his Parisian chateau, as SHE knew that the only real incentive was free airline miles.

9) Politics is largely an old boys' club in which a member bequeaths HIS seat to his son who in turn bequeaths it to his own.

10) The Chicago Bulls are interesting in that they resemble little the docile animal on which ITS name is based.

11) While some say seventeen-years-old is too young to be a wedding dress fashion model, others argue that the population can effectively decide for ITSELF.

12) Sad songs have the seemingly ethereal quality of being able to jettison the bounds of hertz and harmonies and somehow find a reminiscence in the depths of our memories, and then peg THEMSELVES to the depths of our past so that the conscious mind is forced to look back on things long since forgotten.

13) Sad music has the seemingly ethereal quality of being able to jettison the bounds of hertz and harmonies and somehow find a reminiscence in the depths of our memories, and then peg ITSELF to the depths of our past so that the conscious mind is forced to look back on things long since forgotten.

14) We had always known that the dictatorship was evil embodied, that it imprisoned its population, and prohibited the transmission and exchange of outside information, but to find out the depths of ITS misinformation campaign was truly disquieting.

15) The Olympics is an event rich with competition, athleticism, and national pride, but unfortunately, according to recent studies IT DOES not bring the level of economic stimulation to their host countries that the committee would have the hosts believe.

16) My mom and dad have essentially presented the paragon of parenthood, as the former never wavers in understanding, counsel, or generosity, the latter is singularly grounded, offering strength and compassion in such a manner that one wonders if HE is channeling saints of bygone eras.

17) If scent is the sense most strongly tied to memory, then should we not be using IT to more effectively remember facts and dates, not only people and occasions?

18) The term "threepeat" was coined following the Los Angeles Lakers' third victory in which the Lakers snatched victory from HIS opponents using the capable talents of one Kobe Bryant.

19) The World Series is far better planned than the Super Bowl in that ITS games are held partially in each team's stadium, unlike the Super Bowl which is held in an arbitrary third-party's location.

20) Little of what was written, accurate as it were, proved to be useful in my researching the causes of the man's incredible memory. NO ERROR.

The copular is conjugated in the subjunctive "were" expressing doubt.

21) Few of the pages written, accurate as THEY were, proved to be useful in my researching the causes of the man's incredible memory.

The copular is still in the subjunctive, expressing doubt as to the accuracy, but the pronoun refers to multiple pages so must be plural

22) If another pair were to follow suit, it would be difficult for the management to be passive or not to protest ITS departure.

23) A trio of women approached us in the Vegas club, and although we used our best pick-up game, it would not give us phone numbers or hope of a later meet-up. NO ERROR

24) This is not my first rodeo, and this is not the first collection of books I have published, despite my editor's stinging criticism of ITS lack of character development.

25) Families that dine together usually maintain their strength and cohesion long after the children move out to attend schools. NO ERROR

26) Either your book or your glasses will need to be moved lest I drop my book bag down and crush THEM.

Subjects split by "either" assume the quantity of the last one listed, in this case "glasses" which is plural.

27) I challenge you to not drop Economics as a class just because one of your classmates says IT can be difficult to master.

Though "Economics" ends in an "S" it is singular.

28) My dog's favorite toys are often too dirty or too buried for THEIR own good.

Pronoun refers to toys not dog.

29) If you end up eating your toddler's peas and carrots, then they will probably fail to fulfill their primary purpose of child nutrition. NO ERROR

They refers to peas and carrots.

30) The senators' oratory did little to sway the opposing party's intransigent ideals, despite ITS heartfelt appeal to the children of all.

Pronoun refers to oratory, not senators.

31) Christine's bull was disinclined to charge the red flags waved in front of him, and far preferred to sit under a tree and smell the flowers HE would find.

32) Remember that conflicts are never clean, and that when the French invaded Russia, *FRANCE/RUSSIA* ended up retreating in short order only to be plagued by the same years later.

"They" is ambiguous and needs to be replaced by one of the countries.

33) The Lakers and the Spurs will never end up playing one another in the post-season, but each is twice the team that EACH was last season.

34) Charles, Baxter, and Sophie are Springer Spaniels with traditional haircuts, but BAXTER'S/CHARLE'S tail is clipped while the other two have full tails.
"His" is ambiguous.

35) Jeff told Jim that JIM/JEFF was a better attorney when he was attending regular meetings, and that the program has a lower recidivism rate than other forms of recovery. *"He" is ambiguous.*

36) Seth told me that Matt was impressed by SETH'S/ MATT'S OWN self-sufficiency, implying that military school usually had beneficial results that extended beyond the classroom.

37) Realizing that HE would not be the winner, the racecar driver offered his competitor a handshake in friendship.
"He" is ambiguous and should be specified.

38) He thinks about her all the time, but insists that he made the right choice, and that in the end he will be responsible for having saved their lives, though he never expects her to see that. NO ERROR

39) She de-friended him on the social networks and said she'd rather not know of the intricacies of status updates, the depths of his likes and dislikes, and the new relationships THEY relayed back for fear that it would only hurt more acutely.

40) THEY tend not to like us as much since the contributions switched their directions.
"They" is ambiguous and would need to be rewritten to specify.

CHAPTER 10

Pronoun Agreement Errors

This covers the other three ways pronouns will be tested, besides pronoun-antecedent agreement.

Pronouns, as you can see, are one of the most complicated parts-of-speech in the English language. In addition to what was covered in the prior section, pronouns must obey the following constructs:

- Relative Pronoun Errors:
    - People must be referred to with "who," things should be referred to with "that", places "where", times "when."
        - Incorrect: *That is the man that stole a vase.*
        - Correct: *That is the man who stole a vase.*

- Pronoun Case Errors:
    - This is the "me" versus "I" error. It asks you to decide whether you need a subject pronoun or an object pronoun.

        - Incorrect: *Please give the books to either Jon or I the next time you see one of us.*
        - Correct: *Please give the books to either Jon or me the next time you see one of us.*

- The elementary way to tackle these is to reduce the sentence to its basic part and see which sounds right:
  - Example: *Please give the books to either Jon or (I/ME) the next time you see one of us.*
  - Reduce this to: *Please give the books to (I/ME).*
  - Clearly, "me" sounds better.

- But the proper way to do these problems is by asking, "are we dealing with a subject or an object?"
- Subjects require subject pronouns, and likewise, objects require object pronouns.

Pro Tip

A very quick way to figure out if you're dealing with a subject or an object is to check if there is a preposition before the pronoun. If there is, you're dealing with an object, if not, then you are most likely dealing with a subject.

Example: Please give the books to either Jon or (I/ME) the next time you see one of us.

Solution: the preposition "to", which comes before the pronoun, lets us know "Jon or Me" is being acted upon which makes it an object, requiring an object pronoun.

Here is a table detailing the different subject and object pronouns:

Person	*Sing. Subject*	*Sing. Object*	*Plur. Subject*	*Plur. Object*
First	I	Me	We	Us
Second	You	You	N/A	N/A
Third	He/She/It	Him/Her/It	They	Them

- Pronoun gerund errors:
  - This is as easy as keeping pronouns in front of gerunds in the possessive case.
    - Incorrect: *The Judge was tired of the plaintiff's attorney, and was upset with him consistently badgering the witnesses*
    - Correct: *The Judge was tired of the plaintiff's attorney, and was upset with his consistently badgering the witnesses*

Pro Tip:

There are more errors that can happen to pronouns than any other part of speech. The best way to tackle pronouns is to keep a running mental checklists and ask: Agreement, Case, Relative, Gerund. Does it agree with its antecedent? Is the case right? Is it relative? Does it come before a gerund? If it's not one of those errors, then it's fine.

Practice

Most of the following sentences contain a pronoun error. Circle the errant pronoun and write the correct one.

1) Put yourself in the shoes of any of the city's waiters, any one of which, if given the opportunity, would love to be placed in your shoes.

2) If he is the one who intends to be crowned, intends to be the leader, and intends to preside over a population who will be governed by him, then he need be the leader his people expect him to be.

3) The race is a stage race in which the one that is the first to arrive in the place that was previously designated by the race officials, will be the recipient of the thing that was deemed a prize earlier.

4) Mozart was known for producing pieces of music, in Austria, where the spirit of the time was evidenced.

5) Which "which" should we use when we want to describe the wardrobe of a witch that weary wanderings had rendered threadbare by her trips to the sandwich shop called, "Which Wich"?

6) Metacognition, a word which owes its roots to meta meaning beyond, and cognition meaning thought, is the discussion of the process of thought, so when discussing a man, the brain of whom is functioning properly, that has recently stumbled upon a hard question on a test, the process of his thought about his thoughts about the solution would be in the realm of metacognition.

7) Anyone who feels that if so many more students, who we haven't actually admitted, are sitting in on the course than ones we have actually admitted, that the room had to be changed, is likely to agree that the curriculum needs revision.

8) I will give praise to the students, any one of which would be praiseworthy in his or her own right, who can accurately list all the elements on the table in order of atomic mass.

9) That is the jolly fellow who the girl and her entire class now at this point firmly believe to be Santa Clause.

10) That is the jolly fellow whom, the girl and her entire class now at this point firmly believe, is Santa Clause.

11) I wanted to, but we never did receive the pleasure of meeting his business partner whom he said knows how to completely control social situations in his absence.

12) Some make no distinction among the styles of cuisine they choose to consume—often equating Indian food with Italian, and not considering the inherent differences whom each poses.

13) The Olympics, the spirit of the game, and the competitors which elected to attend the games despite political disagreements, coalesced to form a memorable event whose recording was our primary concern.

14) Opening it despite not knowing who was behind the door, who seemed strong and well built at the time, turned out to be a sub-par idea.

15) The judge would not accept the lawyer's method of litigation: him constantly badgering the witness until the man on the stand was forced to escalate.

16) The man with Parkinson's woke at 5 every morning, went for a walk to limber up, and then went to the gym to tone his muscles, claiming that him finding and maintaining stasis in an otherwise degenerative disease was reward enough for his efforts.

17) You claim to be perpetually frustrated, but I'm wondering if you annoying others is really the source of this acrimony: are you the source of your own frustrations, or are they truly exogenous as you claim?

18) Popularity is such an odd double-edged sword in the way that being liked should seemingly produce more friends, but often time produces enemies by way of groups who resent one being popular.

19) Whether it is a midlife crisis or not, you must consider what others will think of you buying such an ostentatious car at this point in your life.

20) The diplomat claimed to understand what his boss's arguing with the bordering country's burgeoning trade embargo supporters was doing, but in the end, him arbitrarily nodding at his boss's comments and proclamations yielded little in the way of assurance to his superior.

21) This exceeding trifling witling, considering ranting criticizing concerning adopting fitting wording being exhibiting transcending learning, was displaying notwithstanding ridiculing, surpassing boasting swelling reasoning, disrespecting correcting erring writing, and touching detecting deceiving arguing during debating.

22) Learning by teaching, the teacher was educating the educators as to the fleeting nature of youth, and the importance of imparting a worthwhile message: if you are doing your best, then your efforts will be rewarded by being rewarding.

23) You racing cars could end with the destruction of your racing car if your car racing skills do not mature.

24) Comparison is easily done: you are better than me at most things but I am taller than you.

25) When you answer the phone, if someone asks for you, and you are the one speaking, then respond, "this is her."

26) The sanitation engineer argued that he far preferred working the early morning routes, as even though it required getting up early and working without my aid, he liked seeing the sunrise more than me.

27) Was it him?

28) Although we do not remember it, it must have been us who knocked over the potted plants in our haste to flee from the impending storm.

29) Now, please point me in the direction of the group that objected to my being here and presenting my findings, but first please tell me it isn't them over there in the corner looking particularly bellicose.

30) I am looking for the alumni meeting; is that them in the corner by the, "go Quakers!" Sign?

31) I would give the appropriate approbation to he who is found in possession of a working knowledge of the different pronoun cases: nominative, objective, possessive.

32) I'm sorry, as I missed the first part of the conversation and the finale of the race; you are faster than who?

33) I'm younger than he, so it should be me who is the first to roll the die.

34) Regarding the two rejected players in the corner: you must agree that I and she far prefer the team composed of Payton and Eli to that composed of he and she.

35) Regarding the two rejected players in the corner: you must agree that he and she far prefer the team composed of Payton and Eli to the team that him and her composed.

36) The male and female administrators of the school were not vindictive in their giving detention to my sister and I, for the punishment that he and she provided to me and her was fair and equitable and commensurate with the crime that he did to her and that she did to him.

37) Some forget that the TV star and her boyfriend formed a band called “him and her”, and that the crowds of people who pay good money to see he and she play him and her classics are considered some of the most diehard fans in the music industry.

38) Men like we are hardened to such criticisms.

39) Men like us, so we are hardened to such criticisms.

40) Be it us who are called to fight the fire or be it the fire brigade of the other city, the fire will be fought by they who are called.

Answers

1) Put yourself in the shoes of any of the city's waiters, any one of WHO, if given the opportunity, would love to be placed in your shoes.

Take out the comma splice to make it easier to determine the best pronoun: "any one of who would love." "Who" is the subject of the verb "love."

2) If he is the one who intends to be crowned, intends to be the leader, and intends to preside over a population WHICH or THAT will be governed by him, then he need be the leader his people expect him to be.

Refer to things (population) with "which" or "that."

3) The race is a stage race in which the one WHO is the first to arrive in the place that was previously designated by the race officials, will be the recipient of the thing that was deemed a prize earlier.

Refer to people (the one) with "who."

4) Mozart was known for producing pieces of music, in Austria, IN WHICH the spirit of the time was evidenced.

"In Austria" is in a comma splice and doesn't pertain to the main clause, so we know that "the spirit of the time was evidenced" must be referring to the music not to Austria.

5) Which "which" should we use when we want to describe a the wardrobe of a witch WHOSE weary wanderings had rendered threadbare by her trips to the sandwich shop, *Which Witch?*

Refer to people (a which) with "who" or "whose."

6) Metacognition, a word which owes its roots to *meta* meaning *beyond*, and *cognition* meaning *thought*, is the discussion of the process of thought, so when discussing a man, the brain of whom is functioning properly, WHO has recently stumbled upon a hard question on a test, the process of his thought about his thoughts about the solution would be in the realm of metacognition.

Take out the comma splices to help you figure out the best pronoun: "so when discussing a man who has recently stumbled."

7) Anyone who feels that if so many more students, WHOM we haven't actually admitted, are sitting in on the course than ones we have actually admitted, that the room had to be changed, is likely to agree that the curriculum needs revision.

Simplify it to "more students whom we admitted." Realize that "students" are the object of "admitted" so it requires an object pronoun.

8) I will give praise to the students, any one of WHO would be praiseworthy in his or her own right, who can accurately list all the elements on the table in order of atomic mass.

"I will give praise to the students" is a separate clause from "any one of who..." Dealing with the second clause you see we're talking about someone who can list the elements. "Any one" is the subject of the second clause, so it requires a subject pronoun: "who."

9) That is the jolly fellow WHOM the girl and her entire class now at this point firmly believe to be Santa Clause.

The subject of the sentence is "the girl and her entire class" so "the jolly fellow" is the object, and must be referred to with object pronouns.

10) That is the jolly fellow WHO, the girl and her entire class now at this point firmly believe, is Santa Clause.

Drop the comma splice and simplify the sentence to "jolly fellow who is Santa Clause."

11) I wanted to, but we never did receive the pleasure of meeting his business partner WHO he said knows how to completely control social situations in his absence.

This can be reduced to "business partner who knows."

12) Some make no distinction among the styles of cuisine they choose to consume—often equating Indian food with Italian, and not considering the inherent differences WHICH each poses.

Refer to things with "which."

13) The Olympics, the spirit of the game, and the competitors which elected to attend the games despite political disagreements, coalesced to form a memorable event whose recording was our primary concern. NO ERROR

The SAT will never test the difference between "that" and "which." It's too obscure and isn't wholly agreed upon by grammarians.

14) Opening it despite not knowing who was behind the door, WHICH seemed strong and well built at the time, turned out to be a sub-par idea.

Refer to things (door) with "which."

15) The judge would not accept the lawyer's method of litigation—HIS constantly badgering the witness until the man on the stand was forced to escalate.

Keep possessive pronouns before gerunds.

16) The man with Parkinson's woke at 5 every morning, went for a walk to limber up, and then went to the gym to tone his muscles, claiming that HIS finding and maintaining stasis in an otherwise degenerative disease was reward enough for his efforts.

Keep possessive pronouns before gerunds.

17) You claim to be perpetually frustrated, but I'm wondering if YOUR annoying others is really the source of this acrimony: are you the source of your own frustrations, or are they truly exogenous as you claim.

Keep possessive pronouns before gerunds.

18) Popularity is such an odd double-edged sword in the way that being liked should seemingly produce more friends, but often time produces enemies by way of groups who resent ONE'S being popular.

Keep possessive pronouns before gerunds.

19) Whether it is a midlife crisis or not, you must consider what others will think of YOUR buying such an ostentatious car at this point in your life.

Keep possessive pronouns before gerunds.

20) The diplomat claimed to understand what his boss's arguing with the bordering country's burgeoning trade embargo supporters was doing, but in the end, HIS arbitrarily nodding at his boss's comments and proclamations yielded little in the way of assurance to his superior.

Keep possessive pronouns before gerunds.

21) This exceeding trifling witling, considering ranting criticizing concerning adopting fitting wording being exhibiting transcending learning, was displaying notwithstanding ridiculing, surpassing boasting swelling reasoning, disrespecting correcting erring writing, and touching detecting deceiving arguing during debating. NO ERROR

22) Learning by teaching, the teacher was educating the educators as to the fleeting nature of youth, and the importance of imparting a worthwhile message: if you are doing your best, then your efforts will be rewarded by being rewarding. NO ERROR

23) YOUR racing cars could end with the destruction of your racing car if your car racing skills do not mature.

Keep possessive pronouns before gerunds.

24) Comparison is easily done: you are better than I at most things but I am taller than you. NO ERROR

When comparing pronouns you should almost always use the subjective form of the pronoun.

Discussion:
In most cases there is an implied verb after the pronoun. I'll concede that this is actually a fairly fractious position, and the correct preposition to follow "than" has been widely debated since the 1800s, but for our purposes, and for the goal of always avoiding ambiguity: follow "than" with a subject or subject pronoun.

Example: you are better than I (am) at most things. You are taller than I (am)

25) When you answer the phone, if someone asks for you, and you are the one speaking, then respond, "this is SHE"

This one is tricky but technically correct. We must follow copular verbs (to be) with subjects.

Discussion:
If you're curious: copular verbs are special. While most verbs can take a passive and active voice, copular verbs cannot. Try to convert "I am" to the passive voice. It would be something like "me was being was by me"—nonsense. That said, the inability of copular verbs to become passive means they can never have things done to them. Because objective pronouns require things to be done to them, and the copular can never impose this meaning, you cannot pair a copular with an object pronoun.

26) The sanitation engineer argued that he far preferred working the early morning routes, as even though it required getting up early and working without my aid, he liked seeing the sunrise more than me.

This is fine, but it would be fine as "I" instead of me as well. The meaning would be different.

27) Was it HE?

Just think: "Was Joe the president?" "Was HE the president?" "Was HE it?"

28) Although we do not remember it, it must have been WE who knocked over the potted plants in our haste to flee from the impending storm.

You can't do this by ear. You need to ask yourself, is "we" the subject or object? Did it have something done to it (making it the object)? Or did it do something (making it the subject)? "We" knocked over the lamp.

29) Now, please point me in the direction of the group that objected to my being here and presenting my findings, but first please tell me it isn't THEY over there in the corner looking particularly bellicose.

This sentence can be simplified like this:

"It is not they, looking particularly bellicose." The modifier "looking particularly bellicose" doesn't have anything to do with the pronoun choice, so just let the sentence be "It is not they." And for the same reason we need to say, "It is I" not "It is me" we have to use the subject pronoun after the copular "to be." So, "It is they" is correct.

30) I am looking for the alumni meeting; is that THEY in the corner by the, "go Quakers!" Sign?

Read the explanations to 29 and 25

31) I would give the appropriate approbation to HIM who is found in possession of a working knowledge of the different pronoun cases: nominative, objective, possessive.

Use the preposition rule "to" right before the pronoun demands an object pronoun.

32) I'm sorry, as I missed the first part of the conversation and the finale of the race; you are faster than who?

No Error

33) I'm younger than he, so it should be I who is the first to roll the die.

If this sounds off, just remember the copular rule "be" goes with subject pronouns.

34) Regarding the two rejected players in the corner: you must agree that I and she far prefer the team composed of Payton and Eli to that composed of HIM AND HER.

Note the preposition "of" before the pronouns.

35) Regarding the two rejected players in the corner: you must agree that he and she far prefer the team composed of Payton and Eli to the team that HE AND SHE composed.

Now "he and she" are subjects and are "composing."

36) The male and female administrators of the school were not vindictive in their giving detention to my sister and I, for the punishment that he and she provided to me and her was fair and equitable and commensurate with the crime that he did to her and that she did to him.

No error.

37) Some forget that the TV star and her boyfriend formed a band called "him and her", and that the crowds of people who pay good money to see HIM AND HER play *him and her* classics are considered some of the most diehard fans in the music industry.

Incidentally, "Him and Her" is the name of a band. But the capitalized instance of the words "Him and Her" are objects that will be seen.

38) Men like US are hardened to such criticisms.

"Like" is a preposition here, so the proper pronoun to use is an object pronoun.

39) Men like US, so we are hardened to such criticisms.

No Error

40) Be it us who are called to fight the fire or be it the fire brigade of the other city, the fire will be fought by THEM who are called.

Preposition before "them" makes the subject pronoun a necessity.

CHAPTER 11

Punctuation

Seemingly easy, punctuation errors are actually one of the most complex topics on the test. The breadth of material alone makes the section daunting. Students must be familiar with all of the following:

- End of sentence punctuation:

Make sure whatever you chose to end the sentence with matches the context. Don't change to an interrogative style (?) when the rest of the passage is declaratory (.).

- Within sentence punctuation:
  For the purposes of the SAT, these are used to break thoughts within sentences (as opposed to add modifiers, or comma splices which will be covered later)

  - Colons: used before a list or an explanation. The most important thing to remember is that what comes before the colon must be able to stand on its own as a complete sentence.
    - Correct: *There is only one thing left to do: sing.*
    - Correct: *The committee is composed of: a baker, a cobbler, and a candlestick maker.*
    - Incorrect: *How exciting: the ships have come home at last.*
    - Incorrect: *Her favorite recipes included: fried shrimp, boiled shrimp, and shrimp gumbo.*

  - Semicolons: used to join two independent clauses. The most important thing to remember is that what comes before and after the semicolon must be complete sentences.
    - Correct: *I like to go swimming; I'll go to the pool this evening*
    - Incorrect: *Because I like to go swimming; I'll go to the pool this evening*

- Dashes: show shifts in tone or direction. A dash is a loose and unconfined punctuation type and it could really do the job of every other form of punctuation, but for the purposes of the SAT, the dash is used to show a sharp divergence in thought, and what comes before the dash must be a complete sentence
    - Example: *I was going to fail—wait, no, I will succeed!*
    - Example: *The car wash literally took the paint off my car—and the man had the audacity to ask for a tip!*

- Items in a series
    - Commas: used when you have more than two items in a series
        - Correct: *I like potatoes, apples, and carrots*
        - Correct: *The man was old, sickly, and cantankerous.*
        - Incorrect: *The man was old, sickly.*
        - Incorrect: *The man was old, and sickly.*

    - Semicolons: semicolons should only be used to separate items if using a comma would be confusing.
        - Incorrect: *The tickets I purchased were for Led Zeppelin, whom I adore, Pink Floyd, which will be a cover band, of course, and The Rolling Stones.* (It becomes difficult to separate the band names from the clauses which follow)
        - Correct: *The tickets I purchased were for Led Zeppelin, whom I adore; Pink Floyd, which will be a cover band, of course; and The rolling Stones.*

- Non-Restrictive and Parenthetical Elements:
  These are simply three different ways to add extra, but non-essential information, to a sentence. They are interchangeable.

    - Commas
        - Correct: *The suspect in the lineup, who is not as tall as I remember, is the one who stole from me.*
    - Parentheses
        - Correct: *The suspect in the lineup (who is not as tall as I remember) is the one who stole from me.*
    - Dashes

- Correct: *The suspect in the lineup—who is not as tall as I remember—is the one who stole from me.*

- Correcting Run-on sentences:

  A run-on sentence is two independent clauses incorrectly joined.

  - Example: *I love my children I will bequest my estate to them.*

  There are four ways to correctly join independent clauses

  - Comma with a coordinating conjunction (for, and, nor, but, or, yet, so):
    - Correct: *I love my children, so I will bequest my estate to them.*
  - Period
    - Correct: *I love my children. I will bequest my estate to them.*
  - Semicolon
    - Correct: *I love my children; I will bequest my estate to them*
  - Subordinating conjunction
    - Correct: *Because I love my children I will bequest my estate to them.*

Practice

Choose the correct version of the following sentences.

1) A) Several friends and I missed the boat tour; and hence we had to attend the cinema outing.

B) I and several friends missed the boat tour, and hence we had to attend the cinema outing.

C) Several friends and I missed the boat tour, and hence we had to attend the cinema outing.

D) Several friends and I missed the boat tour, hence we had to attend the cinema outing.

2) A) The leader was underwhelmed with the equipment available for the outing, a tent, two sleeping bags, and a couple of backpacks.

B) The leader was underwhelmed with the equipment available for the outing: a tent; two sleeping bags; and a couple of backpacks.

C) The leader, underwhelmed with the equipment available for the outing: a tent, two sleeping bags, and a couple of backpacks: planned a different trip.

D) The leader, underwhelmed with the equipment available for the outing—a tent, two sleeping bags, and a couple of backpacks—planned a different trip.

3) A) Looking ahead, we can expect the project to take at least three engineers, and fourteen designers.

B) Looking ahead, we can expect the project to take: at least three engineers and fourteen designers.

C) Looking ahead, we can expect the project to take at least three engineers and fourteen designers.

D) Looking ahead we can expect the project to take at least three engineers and fourteen designers.

4) A) Did you put the book back in it's place, on the small shelf, in the dining room after using it?

B) Did you put the book back in its place, on the small shelf in the dining room, after using it?

C) Did you put the book back in it's place, on the small shelf in the dining room, after using it?

D) Did you put the book back in its place, on the small shelf, in the dining room after using it?

5) A) There are several problems with the proposed corrections: most importantly: the grammar.

B) There are several problems with the proposed corrections; most importantly: the grammar.

C) There are several problems with the proposed corrections, most importantly, the grammar.

D) There are several problems with the proposed corrections: most importantly, the grammar.

6) A) In retrospect, the study, which was the only one completed in November, was completely pointless.

B) In retrospect, the study which was the only one completed in November was completely pointless.

C) In retrospect the study, which was the only one completed in November, was completely pointless.

D) In retrospect, the study, which was the only one completed in November was completely pointless

7) A) Irvine, despite its small size, has an activity for everyone, regardless of your interests and hobbies.

B) Irvine, despite its small size, has an activity for everyone, regardless of their interests and hobbies.

C) Regardless of your interests and hobbies, Irvine, despite its small size, has an activity for everyone.

D) Regardless of his interests and hobbies, Irvine, despite its small size, has an activity for everyone.

8) A) Underwhelmed with: her meager skills, lack of experience, and serious flaws in character, I could not consider her further for the prestigious position of VP for Marketing.

B) Underwhelmed with her meager skills, lack of experience, and serious flaws in character, I could not consider her further for the prestigious position of VP for Marketing.

C) Underwhelmed with her meager skills, lack of experience, and serious flaws in character, I could not consider her further, for the prestigious position of VP for Marketing.

D) Underwhelmed with her meager skills; lack of experience; and serious flaws in character; I could not consider her further for the prestigious position of VP for Marketing.

9) A) One must exercise one's best judgment, in order to move up the ranks at CBS, the premier cable news network on the West Coast

B) One must exercise her best judgment in order to move up the ranks at CBS, the premier cable news network on the West Coast

C) In order to move up the ranks at CBS, the premier cable news network on the West Coast, one must exercise her best judgment.

D) In order to move up the ranks at CBS, the premier cable news network on the West Coast, one must exercise one's best judgment.

10) A) My mom was upset with the noisy, irresponsible dog owner in the yellow, Tudor house across the street.

B) My mom was upset with the noisy, irresponsible dog owner in the yellow Tudor house across the street.

C) My mom was upset with the noisy, irresponsible, dog owner in the yellow, Tudor house across the street.

D) My mom was upset with the noisy irresponsible dog owner in the yellow Tudor house across the street.

11) A) Social Psychology, a branch of Psychology, is the study of how a person's thoughts, feelings, and behaviors are impacted by the presence or perceived presence of others.

B) Social Psychology, a branch of Psychology, is the study of how a person's thoughts, feelings, and behaviors are impacted by the presence, or perceived presence of others.

C) Social Psychology, a branch of Psychology, is the study of how a persons thoughts, feelings, and behaviors are impacted by the presence or perceived presence of others.

D) Social Psychology, a branch of Psychology, is the study of how a person's thoughts, feelings, and behaviors are impacted by the presence, or perceived presence of others.

12) A) Underwater Basket Weaving was my favorite course in college: except for the fact that it met on Fridays at 8AM.

B) Underwater Basket Weaving was my favorite course in college—except for the fact that it met on Fridays—at 8AM.

C) Underwater Basket Weaving was my favorite course in college: except for the fact that it met on Friday's at 8AM.

D) Underwater Basket Weaving was my favorite course in college—except for the fact that it met on Fridays: at 8AM.

13) A) Everyone has their own method for coping with stress—whether it be exercise, consumption of comfort food, or increased use of caffeine.

B) Everyone has his own method for coping with stress, whether it be exercise, consumption of comfort food, or increased use of caffeine.

C) Everyone has his own method for coping with stress—whether it be exercise, consumption of comfort food, or increased use of caffeine.

D) Everyone has their own method for coping with stress; whether it be exercise, consumption of comfort food, or increased use of caffeine.

14) A) Our pets' love is wonderful because they are unconditional, unlike that of a human.

B) Our pet's love are wonderful because it is unconditional, unlike that of a human.

C) Our pets love are wonderful because they are unconditional, unlike that of a human.

D) Our pets' love is wonderful because it is unconditional, unlike that of a human.

15) A) My only son, Charlie, has a much different personality than either of my two daughters; my elder daughter, Cindy is very wise, while my younger daughter, Evelyn is effervescent.

B) My only son, Charlie, has a much different personality than either of my two daughters; my elder daughter Cindy is very wise, while my younger daughter Evelyn is effervescent.

C) My only son Charlie has a much different personality than either of my two daughters; my elder daughter Cindy is very wise, while my younger daughter Evelyn is effervescent.

D) My only son Charlie has a much different personality than either of my two daughters; my elder daughter, Cindy is very wise, while my younger daughter, Evelyn is effervescent.

16) A) In this generation, pop stars are being curated by fans—on sites like YouTube—rather than in the corporate offices of record labels?

B) In this generation, pop stars are being curated by fans—on sites like YouTube, rather than in the corporate offices of record labels?

C) In this generation, pop stars are being curated by fans—on sites like YouTube—rather than in the corporate offices of record labels.

D) In this generation, pop stars are being curated by fans on sites like YouTube, rather than in the corporate offices of record labels.

17) A) Young people, defined as being under age thirty-five, have a huge advantage over older members of the work force in that they are often much more adaptable, and technologically adept.

B) Young people, defined as being under age thirty-five, have a huge advantage over older members of the work force, in that they are often much more adaptable and technologically adept.

C) Young people defined as being under age thirty-five, have a huge advantage over older members of the work force in that they are often much more adaptable and technologically adept.

D) Young people, defined as being under age thirty-five, have a huge advantage over older members of the work force in that they are often much more adaptable and technologically adept.

18) A) So far, no one at try-outs has completed the expected, 25 pull-ups, 200 crunches, and 30 free throws.

B) So far no one at try-outs has completed the expected 25 pull-ups, 200 crunches, and 30 free throws.

C) So far at try-outs: 25 pull-ups, 200 crunches, and 30 free throws have not been completed.

D) So far at try-outs, 25 pull-ups, 200 crunches, and 30 free throws have not been completed.

19) A) She tried forty different chemical formulas for the new, Sourzz candy recipe before she struck the perfect balance of tart and sweet.

B) She tried forty different chemical formulas for the new Sourzz, candy recipe before she struck the perfect balance of tart and sweet.

C) She tried forty different chemical formulas for the new Sourzz candy recipe before she struck the perfect balance of tart and sweet.

D) She tried forty different chemical formulas for the new, Sourzz, candy recipe before she struck the perfect balance of tart and sweet.

20) A) If Congress remains divided, who will push forward new legislation intended to confront the pressing problems of our modern age.

B) If Congress remains divided who will push forward new legislation, intended to confront the pressing problems of our modern age?

C) If Congress remains divided, who will push forward new legislation, intended to confront the pressing problems of our modern age.

D) If Congress remains divided, who will push forward new legislation intended to confront the pressing problems of our modern age?

21) A) Underlying his choice of Marine Biology as his college major, at Penn State, is him yearning for adventure.

B) Underlying his choice of Marine Biology as his college major, at Penn State, is his yearning for adventure.

C) Underlying his choice of Marine Biology as his college major at Penn State, is him yearning for adventure.

D) Underlying his choice of Marine Biology as his college major at Penn State is his yearning for adventure.

22) A) Behind every incredible baseball statistic is: a determined, genetically gifted athlete.

B) Behind every incredible baseball statistic, is a determined, genetically gifted athlete.

C) Behind every incredible baseball statistic is a determined, genetically gifted, athlete.

D) Behind every incredible baseball statistic is a determined, genetically gifted athlete.

23) A) Practicing your musical instruments in a shared, living space, such as an apartment, is discourteous and against the rules.

B) Practicing your musical instruments in a shared living space, such as an apartment, is discourteous and against the rules.

C) Practicing your musical instruments in a shared living space such as an apartment is discourteous and against the rules.

D) Practicing your musical instruments in a shared, living space such as an apartment is discourteous and against the rules.

24) A) Are you, like most environmental scientists, wondering what will be the impact of the ever-increasing world population on the natural resources we depend upon.

B) Are you, like most environmental scientists wondering what will be the impact of the ever-increasing world population on the natural resources we depend upon.

C) Are you, like most environmental scientists, wondering what will be the impact of the ever-increasing world population on the natural resources we depend upon?

D) Are you like most environmental scientists, wondering what will be the impact of the ever-increasing world population on the natural resources we depend upon?

25) A) It's important to note what he still has left to clean up: his socks must be put in their drawer, his baseball cards should be stored in their case, and his bike must be put on its rack.

B) Its important to note what he still has left to clean up: his socks must be put in their drawer; his baseball cards should be stored in their case; and his bike must be put on it's rack.

C) It's important to note what he still has left to clean up: his socks must be put in their drawer; his baseball cards should be stored in their case; and his bike must be put on its rack.

D) Its important to note what he still has left to clean up: his socks must be put in their drawer; his baseball cards should be stored in their case; and his bike must be put on it's rack.

26) A) The contestant who can most quickly determine the mystery phrase will win a prize box, who's contents will not be revealed until the end of the program.

B) The contestant who can most quickly determine the mystery phrase will win a prize box, whose contents will not be revealed until the end of the program.

C) The contestant, who can most quickly determine the mystery phrase, will win a prize box, who's contents will not be revealed until the end of the program.

D) The contestant who can most quickly determine the mystery phrase, will win a prize box, whose contents will not be revealed until the end of the program.

27) A) Sugar-coating the news will not help, because your dog has been hit by a car and killed.

B) Sugar-coating the news will not help, your dog has been hit by a car and killed.

C) Sugar-coating the news will not help: your dog has been hit by a car and killed.

D) Sugar-coating the news will not help: your dog has been hit by a car, and killed.

28) A) I walked to the store and back at least 3 times last week: the path is very beautiful at this time of year.

B) I walked to the store and back at least 3 times last week, the path is very beautiful at this time of year.

C) I walked to the store and back at least 3 times last week on the path which is very beautiful at this time of year.

D) I walked to the store and back—at least 3 times last week—on the path, which is very beautiful at this time of year.

29) A) I sometimes wonder, if there is life, alien or human, on other planets in galaxies far, far away.

B) I sometimes wonder if there is life—alien or human, on other planets in galaxies far, far away.

C) I sometimes wonder, if there is life—alien or human—on other planets, in galaxies far, far away.

D) I sometimes wonder if there is life—alien or human—on other planets, in galaxies far, far away.

30) A) Fortunately, 99% of people have received measles vaccines, which has prevented the outbreak from being much worse than it currently is.

B) Fortunately, 99% of people have received measles vaccines, preventing the outbreak from being much worse than it currently is.

C) Fortunately, 99% of people have received measles vaccines: which has prevented the outbreak from being much worse than it currently is.

D) Fortunately, 99% of people have received measles vaccines; preventing the outbreak from being much worse than it currently is.

For problems 31-40, choose the *incorrect* sentence:

31) A) Owls come out at night—when other animals are sleeping—to do their hunting and nest building.

B) Owls come out at night when other animals are sleeping to do their hunting and nest building.

C) Owls come out at night, when other animals are sleeping, to do their hunting and nest building.

D) Owls come out at night when other animals are sleeping, to do their hunting and nest building.

32) A) Surprisingly, many brilliant researchers—including the famous Albert Einstein—had more failures than successes.

B) Surprisingly, many brilliant researchers, including the most famous physicist of the twentieth century Albert Einstein, had more failures than successes.

C) Surprisingly, many brilliant researchers had more failures than successes, including the most famous physicist of the twentieth century, Albert Einstein.

D) Surprisingly, many brilliant researchers had more failures than successes—including the famous Albert Einstein.

33) A) One's purpose in life is left to his own discretion.

B) Her purpose in life is left to her own discretion.

C) One's purpose in life is left to one's own discretion.

D) Should one's purpose in life be left to another's discretion?

34) A) Studying abroad is a good experience for most college students, especially when they take the proper safety precautions before embarking.

B) Studying abroad is a good experience for most college students, however it is important to take the proper safety precautions before embarking.

C) Studying abroad is a good experience for most college students, but it is important to take the proper safety precautions before embarking.

D) Studying abroad is a good experience for most college students; however, it is important to take the proper safety precautions before embarking.

35) A) Last Thursday it was forecast to rain all day; therefore I grabbed an umbrella before leaving.

B) Last Thursday's forecast was rain, so I grabbed an umbrella before leaving.

C) Last Thursday it was forecast to rain all day, therefore I grabbed an umbrella before leaving.

D) Last Thursday's forecast was rainy, inducing me to grab an umbrella before leaving.

36) A) International Man of Mystery, Austin Powers, was eventually able to defeat Dr. Evil with a stunning composition of daring, wits, and just plain good luck.

B) International Man of Mystery, Austin Powers, was eventually able to defeat Dr. Evil with a stunning composition: daring, wits, and just plain good luck.

C) International Man of Mystery, Austin Powers, was eventually able to defeat Dr. Evil, with a stunning composition of: daring, wits, and just plain good luck.

D) International Man of Mystery, Austin Powers, was eventually able to defeat Dr. Evil with a stunning composition—daring, wits, and just plain good luck.

37) A) Because so many fans visited the memorial for the deceased opera singer, her estate has decided to build another on the East Coast.

B) So many fans visited the memorial for the deceased opera singer that her estate has decided to build another on the East Coast.

C) Many fans visited the memorial for the deceased opera singer; her estate has decided to build another on the East Coast.

D) So many fans visited the memorial for the deceased opera singer, that her estate has decided to build another on the East Coast.

38) A) Since school has not started yet, and will not for another month, I will put my time to good use reading the history textbook in advance.

B) Since school has not started yet, and will not for another month, I will put my time to good use: I will read the history textbook in advance.

C) Since school has not started yet, and will not for another month, I will put my time to good use by reading the history textbook in advance.

D) Since school has not started yet, and will not for another month, I will put my time to good use; reading the history textbook in advance seems to be a good idea.

39) A) There were over a thousand different flowers planted in the garden, the most beautiful part of the palace.

B) The garden was the most beautiful part of the palace, as there were over a thousand different flowers planted there.

C) The garden was the most beautiful part of the palace: there were over a thousand different flowers planted there.

D) There were over a thousand different flowers planted in the garden which was the most beautiful part of the palace.

40) A) In terms of fairy-tales, my favorite is Cinderella—the one where the lowly maid magically transforms into a princess.

B) In terms of fairy-tales, my favorite is Cinderella, the one where the lowly maid magically transforms into a princess.

C) In terms of fairy-tales, my favorite is Cinderella, where the lowly maid magically transforms into a princess.

D) In terms of fairy-tales, my favorite is Cinderella: the one where the lowly maid magically transforms into a princess.

Answers

1) A) Several friends and I missed the boat tour; and hence we had to attend the cinema outing.

B) I and several friends missed the boat tour, and hence we had to attend the cinema outing.

C) Several friends and I missed the boat tour, and hence we had to attend the cinema outing.

D) Several friends and I missed the boat tour, hence we had to attend the cinema outing.

2) A) The leader was underwhelmed with the equipment available for the outing, a tent, two sleeping bags, and a couple of backpacks.

B) The leader was underwhelmed with the equipment available for the outing: a tent; two sleeping bags; and a couple of backpacks.

C) The leader, underwhelmed with the equipment available for the outing: a tent, two sleeping bags, and a couple of backpacks: planned a different trip.

D) The leader, underwhelmed with the equipment available for the outing—a tent, two sleeping bags, and a couple of backpacks—planned a different trip.

3) A) Looking ahead, we can expect the project to take at least three engineers, and fourteen designers.

B) Looking ahead, we can expect the project to take: at least three engineers and fourteen designers.

C) Looking ahead, we can expect the project to take at least three engineers and fourteen designers.

D) Looking ahead we can expect the project to take at least three engineers and fourteen designers.

4) A) Did you put the book back in it's place, on the small shelf, in the dining room after using it?

B) Did you put the book back in its place, on the small shelf in the dining room, after using it?

C) Did you put the book back in it's place, on the small shelf in the dining room, after using it?

D) Did you put the book back in its place, on the small shelf, in the dining room after using it?

5) A) There are several problems with the proposed corrections: most importantly: the grammar.

B) There are several problems with the proposed corrections; most importantly: the grammar.

C) There are several problems with the proposed corrections, most importantly, the grammar.

D) There are several problems with the proposed corrections: most importantly, the grammar.

6) **A) In retrospect, the study, which was the only one completed in November, was completely pointless.**

B) In retrospect, the study which was the only one completed in November was completely pointless.

C) In retrospect the study, which was the only one completed in November, was completely pointless.

D) In retrospect, the study, which was the only one completed in November was completely pointless

7) A) Irvine, despite its small size, has an activity for everyone, regardless of your interests and hobbies.

B) Irvine, despite its small size, has an activity for everyone, regardless of their interests and hobbies.

C) Regardless of your interests and hobbies, Irvine, despite its small size, has an activity for everyone.

D) Regardless of his interests and hobbies, Irvine, despite its small size, has an activity for everyone.

8) A) Underwhelmed with: her meager skills, lack of experience, and serious flaws in character, I could not consider her further for the prestigious position of VP for Marketing.

B) Underwhelmed with her meager skills, lack of experience, and serious flaws in character, I could not consider her further for the prestigious position of VP for Marketing.

C) Underwhelmed with her meager skills, lack of experience, and serious flaws in character, I could not consider her further, for the prestigious position of VP for Marketing.

D) Underwhelmed with her meager skills; lack of experience; and serious flaws in character; I could not consider her further for the prestigious position of VP for Marketing.

9) A) One must exercise one's best judgment, in order to move up the ranks at CBS, the premier cable news network on the West Coast

B) One must exercise her best judgment in order to move up the ranks at CBS, the premier cable news network on the West Coast

C) In order to move up the ranks at CBS, the premier cable news network on the West Coast, one must exercise her best judgment.

D) In order to move up the ranks at CBS, the premier cable news network on the West Coast, one must exercise one's best judgment.

10) A) My mom was upset with the noisy, irresponsible dog owner in the yellow, Tudor house across the street.

B) My mom was upset with the noisy, irresponsible dog owner in the yellow Tudor house across the street.

C) My mom was upset with the noisy, irresponsible, dog owner in the yellow, Tudor house across the street.

D) My mom was upset with the noisy irresponsible dog owner in the yellow Tudor house across the street.

11) **A) Social Psychology, a branch of Psychology, is the study of how a person's thoughts, feelings, and behaviors are impacted by the presence or perceived presence of others.**

B) Social Psychology, a branch of Psychology, is the study of how a person's thoughts, feelings, and behaviors are impacted by the presence, or perceived presence of others.

C) Social Psychology, a branch of Psychology, is the study of how a persons thoughts, feelings, and behaviors are impacted by the presence or perceived presence of others.

D) Social Psychology, a branch of Psychology, is the study of how a person's thoughts, feelings, and behaviors are impacted by the presence, or perceived presence of others.

12) **A) Underwater Basket Weaving was my favorite course in college: except for the fact that it met on Fridays at 8AM.**

B) Underwater Basket Weaving was my favorite course in college—except for the fact that it met on Fridays—at 8AM.

C) Underwater Basket Weaving was my favorite course in college: except for the fact that it met on Friday's at 8AM.

D) Underwater Basket Weaving was my favorite course in college—except for the fact that it met on Fridays: at 8AM.

13) A) Everyone has their own method for coping with stress—whether it be exercise, consumption of comfort food, or increased use of caffeine.

B) Everyone has his own method for coping with stress, whether it be exercise, consumption of comfort food, or increased use of caffeine.

C) Everyone has his own method for coping with stress—whether it be exercise, consumption of comfort food, or increased use of caffeine.

D) Everyone has their own method for coping with stress; whether it be exercise, consumption of comfort food, or increased use of caffeine.

14) A) Our pets' love is wonderful because they are unconditional, unlike that of a human.

B) Our pet's love are wonderful because it is unconditional, unlike that of a human.

C) Our pets love are wonderful because they are unconditional, unlike that of a human.

D) Our pets' love is wonderful because it is unconditional, unlike that of a human.

15) A) My only son, Charlie, has a much different personality than either of my two daughters; my elder daughter, Cindy is very wise, while my younger daughter, Evelyn is effervescent.

B) My only son, Charlie, has a much different personality than either of my two daughters; my elder daughter Cindy is very wise, while my younger daughter Evelyn is effervescent.

C) My only son Charlie has a much different personality than either of my two daughters; my elder daughter Cindy is very wise, while my younger daughter Evelyn is effervescent.

D) My only son Charlie has a much different personality than either of my two daughters; my elder daughter, Cindy is very wise, while my younger daughter, Evelyn is effervescent.

16) A) In this generation, pop stars are being curated by fans—on sites like YouTube—rather than in the corporate offices of record labels?

B) In this generation, pop stars are being curated by fans—on sites like YouTube, rather than in the corporate offices of record labels?

C) In this generation, pop stars are being curated by fans—on sites like YouTube—rather than in the corporate offices of record labels.

D) In this generation, pop stars are being curated by fans on sites like YouTube, rather than in the corporate offices of record labels.

17) A) Young people, defined as being under age thirty-five, have a huge advantage over older members of the work force in that they are often much more adaptable, and technologically adept.

B) Young people, defined as being under age thirty-five, have a huge advantage over older members of the work force, in that they are often much more adaptable and technologically adept.

C) Young people defined as being under age thirty-five, have a huge advantage over older members of the work force in that they are often much more adaptable and technologically adept.

D) Young people, defined as being under age thirty-five, have a huge advantage over older members of the work force in that they are often much more adaptable and technologically adept.

18) A) So far, no one at try-outs has completed the expected, 25 pull-ups, 200 crunches, and 30 free throws.

B) So far no one at try-outs has completed the expected 25 pull-ups, 200 crunches, and 30 free throws.

C) So far at try-outs: 25 pull-ups, 200 crunches, and 30 free throws have not been completed.

D) So far at try-outs, 25 pull-ups, 200 crunches, and 30 free throws have not been completed.

19) A) She tried forty different chemical formulas for the new, Sourzz candy recipe before she struck the perfect balance of tart and sweet.

B) She tried forty different chemical formulas for the new Sourzz, candy recipe before she struck the perfect balance of tart and sweet.

C) She tried forty different chemical formulas for the new Sourzz candy recipe before she struck the perfect balance of tart and sweet.

D) She tried forty different chemical formulas for the new, Sourzz, candy recipe before she struck the perfect balance of tart and sweet.

20) A) If Congress remains divided, who will push forward new legislation intended to confront the pressing problems of our modern age.

B) If Congress remains divided who will push forward new legislation, intended to confront the pressing problems of our modern age?

C) If Congress remains divided, who will push forward new legislation, intended to confront the pressing problems of our modern age.

D) If Congress remains divided, who will push forward new legislation intended to confront the pressing problems of our modern age?

21) A) Underlying his choice of Marine Biology as his college major, at Penn State, is him yearning for adventure.

B) Underlying his choice of Marine Biology as his college major, at Penn State, is his yearning for adventure.

C) Underlying his choice of Marine Biology as his college major at Penn State, is him yearning for adventure.

D) Underlying his choice of Marine Biology as his college major at Penn State is his yearning for adventure.

22) A) Behind every incredible baseball statistic is: a determined, genetically gifted athlete.

B) Behind every incredible baseball statistic, is a determined, genetically gifted athlete.

C) Behind every incredible baseball statistic is a determined, genetically gifted, athlete.

D) Behind every incredible baseball statistic is a determined, genetically gifted athlete.

23) A) Practicing your musical instruments in a shared, living space, such as an apartment, is discourteous and against the rules.

B) Practicing your musical instruments in a shared living space, such as an apartment, is discourteous and against the rules.

C) Practicing your musical instruments in a shared living space such as an apartment is discourteous and against the rules.

D) Practicing your musical instruments in a shared, living space such as an apartment is discourteous and against the rules.

24) A) Are you, like most environmental scientists, wondering what will be the impact of the ever-increasing world population on the natural resources we depend upon.

B) Are you, like most environmental scientists wondering what will be the impact of the ever-increasing world population on the natural resources we depend upon.

C) Are you, like most environmental scientists, wondering what will be the impact of the ever-increasing world population on the natural resources we depend upon?

D) Are you like most environmental scientists, wondering what will be the impact of the ever-increasing world population on the natural resources we depend upon?

25) A) It's important to note what he still has left to clean up: his socks must be put in their drawer, his baseball cards should be stored in their case, and his bike must be put on its rack.

B) Its important to note what he still has left to clean up: his socks must be put in their drawer; his baseball cards should be stored in their case; and his bike must be put on it's rack.

C) It's important to note what he still has left to clean up: his socks must be put in their drawer; his baseball cards should be stored in their case; and his bike must be put on its rack.

D) Its important to note what he still has left to clean up: his socks must be put in their drawer; his baseball cards should be stored in their case; and his bike must be put on it's rack.

26) A) The contestant who can most quickly determine the mystery phrase will win a prize box, who's contents will not be revealed until the end of the program.

B) The contestant who can most quickly determine the mystery phrase will win a prize box, whose contents will not be revealed until the end of the program.

C) The contestant, who can most quickly determine the mystery phrase, will win a prize box, who's contents will not be revealed until the end of the program.

D) The contestant who can most quickly determine the mystery phrase, will win a prize box, whose contents will not be revealed until the end of the program.

27) A) Sugar-coating the news will not help, because your dog has been hit by a car and killed.

B) Sugar-coating the news will not help, your dog has been hit by a car and killed.

C) Sugar-coating the news will not help: your dog has been hit by a car and killed.

D) Sugar-coating the news will not help: your dog has been hit by a car, and killed.

28) **A) I walked to the store and back at least 3 times last week: the path is very beautiful at this time of year.**

B) I walked to the store and back at least 3 times last week, the path is very beautiful at this time of year.

C) I walked to the store and back at least 3 times last week on the path which is very beautiful at this time of year.

D) I walked to the store and back—at least 3 times last week—on the path, which is very beautiful at this time of year.

29) A) I sometimes wonder, if there is life, alien or human, on other planets in galaxies far, far away.

B) I sometimes wonder if there is life—alien or human, on other planets in galaxies far, far away.

C) I sometimes wonder, if there is life—alien or human—on other planets, in galaxies far, far away.

D) I sometimes wonder if there is life—alien or human—on other planets, in galaxies far, far away.

30) **A) Fortunately, 99% of people have received measles vaccines, which has prevented the outbreak from** being much worse than it currently is.

B) Fortunately, 99% of people have received measles vaccines, preventing the outbreak from being much worse than it currently is.

C) Fortunately, 99% of people have received measles vaccines: which has prevented the outbreak from being much worse than it currently is.

D) Fortunately, 99% of people have received measles vaccines; preventing the outbreak from being much worse than it currently is.

For problems 31-40, choose the incorrect sentence:

31) A) Owls come out at night—when other animals are sleeping—to do their hunting and nest building.

B) Owls come out at night when other animals are sleeping to do their hunting and nest building.

C) Owls come out at night, when other animals are sleeping, to do their hunting and nest building.

D) Owls come out at night when other animals are sleeping, to do their hunting and nest building.

32) A) Surprisingly, many brilliant researchers—including the famous Albert Einstein—had more failures than successes.

B) Surprisingly, many brilliant researchers, including the most famous physicist of the twentieth century Albert Einstein, had more failures than successes.

C) Surprisingly, many brilliant researchers had more failures than successes, including the most famous physicist of the twentieth century, Albert Einstein.

D) Surprisingly, many brilliant researchers had more failures than successes—including the famous Albert Einstein.

33) **A) One's purpose in life is left to his own discretion.**

B) Her purpose in life is left to her own discretion.

C) One's purpose in life is left to one's own discretion.

D) Should one's purpose in life be left to another's discretion?

34) A) Studying abroad is a good experience for most college students, especially when they take the proper safety precautions before embarking.

B) Studying abroad is a good experience for most college students, however it is important to take the proper safety precautions before embarking.

C) Studying abroad is a good experience for most college students, but it is important to take the proper safety precautions before embarking.

D) Studying abroad is a good experience for most college students; however, it is important to take the proper safety precautions before embarking.

35) A) Last Thursday it was forecast to rain all day; therefore I grabbed an umbrella before leaving.

B) Last Thursday's forecast was rain, so I grabbed an umbrella before leaving.

C) Last Thursday it was forecast to rain all day, therefore I grabbed an umbrella before leaving.

D) Last Thursday's forecast was rainy, inducing me to grab an umbrella before leaving.

36) A) International Man of Mystery, Austin Powers, was eventually able to defeat Dr. Evil with a stunning composition of daring, wits, and just plain good luck.

B) International Man of Mystery, Austin Powers, was eventually able to defeat Dr. Evil with a stunning composition: daring, wits, and just plain good luck.

C) International Man of Mystery, Austin Powers, was eventually able to defeat Dr. Evil, with a stunning composition of: daring, wits, and just plain good luck.

D) International Man of Mystery, Austin Powers, was eventually able to defeat Dr. Evil with a stunning composition—daring, wits, and just plain good luck.

37) A) Because so many fans visited the memorial for the deceased opera singer, her estate has decided to build another on the East Coast.

B) So many fans visited the memorial for the deceased opera singer that her estate has decided to build another on the East Coast.

C) Many fans visited the memorial for the deceased opera singer; her estate has decided to build another on the East Coast.

D) So many fans visited the memorial for the deceased opera singer, that her estate has decided to build another on the East Coast.

38) **A) Since school has not started yet, and will not for another month, I will put my time to good use reading the history textbook in advance.**

B) Since school has not started yet, and will not for another month, I will put my time to good use: I will read the history textbook in advance.

C) Since school has not started yet, and will not for another month, I will put my time to good use by reading the history textbook in advance.

D) Since school has not started yet, and will not for another month, I will put my time to good use; reading the history textbook in advance seems to be a good idea.

39) A) There were over a thousand different flowers planted in the garden, the most beautiful part of the palace.

B) The garden was the most beautiful part of the palace, as there were over a thousand different flowers planted there.

C) The garden was the most beautiful part of the palace: there were over a thousand different flowers planted there.

D) There were over a thousand different flowers planted in the garden which was the most beautiful part of the palace.

40) A) In terms of fairy-tales, my favorite is Cinderella—the one where the lowly maid magically transforms into a princess.

B) In terms of fairy-tales, my favorite is Cinderella, the one where the lowly maid magically transforms into a princess.

C) In terms of fairy-tales, my favorite is Cinderella, where the lowly maid magically transforms into a princess.

D) In terms of fairy-tales, my favorite is Cinderella: the one where the lowly maid magically transforms into a princess.

CHAPTER 12

Subject Verb Agreement

This is the pillar of English grammar, and while not difficult to correct, is very difficult to spot because of how relaxed the vernacular has become.

At its core, subject-verb agreement is very easy. The SAT likes to stick with the present tense, which means we can use the "S-Rule."

- S-Rule: either the subject or the verb must end in an "S", but not both, nor neither.
  - Correct: The dog(no "S") runS
  - Correct: The dogS run(no "S")
  - Incorrect: The dogS runS
  - Incorrect: The dog(no "S") run(no "S")

This gets more complicated when you're unsure what the subject of the sentence is. Remember a few rules to help you decide what the subject is:

- The subject comes before the preposition:
  - A bouquet of flowers ("bouquet" is the subject; "of" is the preposition)
  - The piano behind the walnut table was beautiful ("piano" is the subject; "behind" is the preposition)
- When you see "or" only deal with the subject that sits closest to the verb
  - A dog or cats (cats is the subject) run home when they hear the bell ring.
  - Cats or a dog (dog is now the subject) runs home when it hears the bell ring.
- When you see "and" treat it as a plural subject
  - A dog and a cat (treat this as "they") run home

Practice

Many of the sentences below contain misconjugated verbs. Circle the incorrect verb and write in the correct one.

1) The reason for the dog's incessant barking seem to be unrelated to the excuse the owner insists on providing.

2) The reason for the dogs' incessant barking seem to be unrelated to the excuse the owner insists on providing.

3) A bouquet of flowers or a bag of oranges were the two items I was debating bringing to the housewarming party.

4) Ten years of penitence, aside from inuring the man to the challenges of solitude, was revealed as completely without cause when the defense won the appeal, thus exonerating the ex-convict.

5) The amount of time, a spell over which centuries have come and gone, and empires have risen and fallen, wash over us like a wave from the ocean of ages.

6) Mothers of sons of men of the youth of the friends of the group, The Daughters of the American Revolution has generously dedicated this plaque in honor of the first centennial anniversary of the first time the first shot had been fired in the first battlefield of the first war of independence of the United States of America.

7) A mother of sons of men of the youth of the friends of the group, The Daughters of the American Revolution has generously dedicated this plaque in honor of the first centennial anniversary of the first time the first shot had been fired in the first battlefield of the first war of independence of the United States of America.

8) Decide the fate of the children: whether it is their fate to become dentists or whether they are to become a pop music duo, composed of twins, that sing on the major concert circuit in the country is yours to decide.

9) The Los Angeles Lakers, agile, young, and strong of heart, were the frontrunners for the playoffs

10) The World Series that pitted two countries in a win-or-go-home single game, replete with baseball allstars from such far off places as Japan and Cuba, are predicted to last for three days.

11) The woman asked if the criteria by which her paper had been graded was not slanted slightly toward those for whom English was their first language.

12) The number of cars in the parking lot are increasing sharply by the hour, and causes concern for the owner of the lot, who had promised that he had a surfeit of capacity.

13) Do not count the time, she said, for the seconds of the minutes of the hour that will sift through our awareness before my return is unworthy of our notice.

14) Notice that the dog never strays far from its mother and father in the early stages of its life, but leave without hesitation as it matures and develops its own cohort.

15) Some of the sum total of the proceeds of the event is given to charities in the tristate area.

16) Some of the money raised by the government's Quantitative Easing programs are used to buy long-duration treasury notes, in the 20-30 year range.

17) Badgers badgers badger badgers badgers badgered by other badgers.

18) If you are not one of those in the groups of students who forget his or her homework on a regular basis, then you need not worry about the warning.

19) I cannot speak for those who chose to forge their own paths through the endless night, but I can promise to anyone, nationals and immigrants, who come to fight with me will be rewarded with riches beyond belief.

20) Each of the groups of racers know that the track is perilous and that it poses risks, even in the most benign of conditions.

21) Last week, the grand jury announced that the former city manager as well as his brothers are sentenced to six consecutive life sentences.

22) Twelve dogs or a very uncomfortable cat is responsible for the noise last night.

23) Neither the Oklahoma City Thunder nor the LA Lakers pose a great threat to NBA-imposed salary caps.

24) The sports media drones incessantly about dehydration and the benefits of this sports drink over that, but truthfully, either are sufficient to quench my thirst.

25) There are a multitude of reasons why I cannot go with you to the prom, but none more pressing than your lack of a car.

26) Here are two teams: both equally lacking in fortitude and prowess, and neither take enough time to strengthen its core skills.

27) Beside the wall lay a basket of muffins which were specially prepared for you to take with you on your picnic.

28) Intermittently exist a need for campaign finance reform, but seemingly only in years when the other party has the majority.

29) Remaining to be seen are a team of teamsters or a union of prop masters, so it is pretty unlikely that the movie will wrap on schedule.

30) The president but not his cabinet members have submitted nominations for the chief-justice of the Supreme Court.

31) A non-negligible percentage of actors, regardless of individual country of origin, partake of the Japanese delicacy, sashimi.

32) The candidate was dynamic and a gifted public speaker, but even as such, a large percentage of senior citizens are voting against her.

33) Looking at the damage, the doctor estimates that the percentage of the patient's body covered by burns are almost 50%.

34) When completing simple math, it is important to remember the simple premise: one and one are two.

35) Parliamentary procedure is wrought with inefficiencies, as in the case of disagreements: if the prime minister but not the council members want to pass a resolution, then it would go back to the committee.

36) Please tell me your brother is not one of those people who, so eagerly, has sprinted headlong into the radical movement.

37) I know which book you are talking about, but this is not one of those Drug Store Novels, so many of which do not warrant the death of a tree for their printing, which deals with the subject of long lost love.

38) I only posit that Einstein, being the one who brought us the two pillars of physics, is one of the greatest mathematicians who has ever lived.

39) How are we supposed to find our way out of the labyrinth when none of us know our cardinal directions?

40) Buffalo buffalo Buffalo buffalo buffalos buffalo Buffalo buffalo. (Hint: “buffalo” is a verb meaning, to intimidate)

Answers

1) The reason for the dog's incessant barking SEEMS to be unrelated to the excuse the owner insists on providing.

   Reason seems.

2) The reason for the dogs' incessant barking SEEMS to be unrelated to the excuse the owner insists on providing.

   Reason seems.

3) A bouquet of flowers or a bag of oranges WAS the two items I was debating bringing to the housewarming party.

   A bag was.

4) Ten years of penitence, aside from inuring the man to the challenges of solitude, WERE revealed as completely without cause when the defense won the appeal, thus exonerating the ex-convict.

   Ten years were.

5) The amount of time, a spell over which centuries have come and gone, and empires have risen and fallen, WASHES over us like a wave from the ocean of ages.

   The amount washes.

6) Mothers of sons of men of the youth of the friends of the group, The Daughters of the American Revolution HAVE generously dedicated this plaque in honor of the first centennial anniversary of the first time the first shot had been fired in the first battle field of the first war of independence of the United States of America.

   Mothers have.

7) A mother of sons of men of the youth of the friends of the group, The Daughters of the American Revolution has generously dedicated this plaque in honor of the first centennial anniversary of the first time the first shot had been fired in the first battle field of the first war of independence of the United States of America. NO ERROR

   A mother has.

8) Decide the fate of the children: whether it is their fate to become dentists or whether they are to become a pop music duo, composed of twins, that SINGS on the major concert circuit in the country is yours to decide.

   A duo that sings.

9) The Los Angeles Lakers, agile, young, and strong of heart, were the frontrunners for the playoffs

   The Lakers (singular subject despite ending in "S") was.

10) The World Series that pitted two countries in a win-or-go-home single game, replete with baseball allstars from such far off places as Japan and Cuba, IS predicted to last for three days.

World Series (singular subject) is.

11) The woman asked if the criteria by which her paper had been graded WERE not slanted slightly toward those for whom English was their first language.

Criteria (a plural subject; the singular of "criteria" is "criterion") were.

12) The number of cars in the parking lot IS increasing sharply by the hour, and causes concern for the owner of the lot, who had promised that he had a surfeit of capacity.

The number is.

13) Do not count the time, she said, for the seconds of the minutes of the hour that will sift through our awareness before my return ARE unworthy of our notice.

The seconds are.

14) Notice that the dog never strays far from its mother and father in the early stages of its life, but LEAVES without hesitation as it matures and develops its own cohort.

The dog leaves.

15) Some of the sum total of the proceeds of the event is given to charities in the tri-state area. NO ERROR

Some is a strange pronoun which is not itself a subject. The thing that comes after the preposition actually dictates the subject. So "the sum total is given."

This is an exception to the rule which says whatever comes before the preposition is the subject.

16) Some of the money raised by the government's Quantitative Easing programs IS used to buy long-duration treasury notes, in the 20-30 year range.

Again, "money is." See 15 for an explanation.

17) Badgers badgers badger BADGER badgers badgered by other badgers.

This isn't a joke. Badgers are an animal, but the verb "to badger" also means to berate. To make this easier, you can say

Badgers that (other) badgers badger (berate), badger (berate) badgers badgered (berated) by other badgers.

18) If you are not one of those in the groups of students who FORGETS his or her homework on a regular basis, then you need not worry about the warning.

One forgets

19) I cannot speak for those who chose to forge their own paths through the endless night, but I can promise to anyone, nationals and immigrants, who COMES to fight with me will be rewarded with riches beyond belief.

Anyone comes

20) Each of the groups of racers KNOWS that the track is perilous and that it poses risks, even in the most benign of conditions.

Each knows

21) Last week, the grand jury announced that the former city manager as well as his brothers are sentenced to six consecutive life sentences. NO ERROR

22) Twelve dogs or a very uncomfortable cat is responsible for the noise last night. NO ERROR *Deal with the subject closest to the verb: "cat" in this case.*

23) Neither the Oklahoma City Thunder nor the LA Lakers POSES a great threat to NBA-imposed salary caps.

Lakers (a singular, collective proper noun) poses.

24) The sports media drones incessantly about dehydration and the benefits of this sports drink over that, but truthfully, either IS sufficient to quench my thirst.

Either drink is

25) There IS a multitude of reasons why I cannot go with you to the prom, but none more pressing than your lack of a car.

It's always a bit tricky when the subject comes after the verb, but the preposition rule still applies: "multitude" comes before "of." So "a multitude" (singular) is our subject and requires a singular verb.

26) Here are two teams: both equally lacking in fortitude and prowess, and neither TAKES enough time to strengthen its core skills.

Neither (team) takes.

27) Beside the wall LAYS a basket of muffins which were specially prepared for you to take with you on your picnic.

Again, subject after verb: a basket lays

28) Intermittently EXISTS a need for campaign finance reform, but seemingly only in years when the other party has the majority.

A need exists.

29) Remaining to be seen IS a team of teamsters or a union of prop masters, so it is pretty unlikely that the movie will wrap on schedule.

A team is remaining.

30) The president but not his cabinet members HAS submitted nominations for the chief-justice of the Supreme Court.

The president has.

31) A non-negligible percentage of actors, regardless of individual country of origin, PARTAKES of the Japanese delicacy, sashimi.

A percentage partakes.

32) The candidate was dynamic and a gifted public speaker, but even as such, a large percentage of senior citizens IS voting against her.

A percentage is.

33) Looking at the damage, the doctor estimates that the percentage of the patient's body covered by burns IS almost 50%.

The percentage is.

34) When completing simple math, it is important to remember the simple premise: one and one are two. NO ERROR

"One and one" can be thought of as a compound subject, requiring a plural verb. The ear wants the correct version to be "one and one is two" because you want "and" to be a verb meaning, "plus." But it is not.

35) Parliamentary procedure is wrought with inefficiencies, as in the case of disagreements: if the prime minister but not the council members WANTS to pass a resolution, then it would go back to the committee.

Prime minister wants.

36) Please tell me your brother is not one of those people who, so eagerly, has sprinted headlong into the radical movement. NO ERROR

One has sprinted.

37) I know which book you are talking about, but this is not one of those Drug Store Novels, so many of which do not warrant the death of a tree for their printing, which deals with the subject of long-lost love. NO ERROR

One of those which deals.

38) I only posit that Einstein, being the one who brought us the two pillars of physics, is one of the greatest mathematicians who has ever lived. NO ERROR

One has.

39) How are we supposed to find our way out of the labyrinth when none of us know our cardinal directions NO ERROR

"none" is a special pronoun, like "some" which needs to see what comes after it in order to know if it is singular or plural. Because this "none" refers to "us" it means "not any" so it requires a plural verb.

40) Buffalo buffalo Buffalo buffalo BUFFALO buffalo Buffalo buffalo. (Hint: buffalo is a verb meaning, to intimidate)

This sentence is a classic. It hinges on the fact that you don't need the words "that" to make a complete sentence.
Here's the explanation:

Buffalo buffalo (the animal from the city of Buffalo) (THAT OTHER) Buffalo buffalo (animals from the city of Buffalo) buffalo (meaning bother)(THEMSELVES) buffalo (meaning bother) Buffalo buffalo (animals from the city of Buffalo)

It's like saying "New York people that New York people bother, they themselves, bother New York people."

At any rate, the subject is plural so it needs a plural verb.

CHAPTER 13

Usage

Usage errors test your ability to use the correct versions of words—no small task considering so many English words are homophones (*their* and *there*)or near-homophones (*noisome* and *noisy*).

Usage errors come in two varieties: homophones and wrong-definitions.

- Homophone errors attempt to trick you by playing to your sense of "sounding right"
    - Example: *I am not use to this kind of treatment.*

      If you read that aloud you would never spot the error. But a keen eye will realize that the proper phrase is "used to" not "use to."

    - Example: *The ascent of each of the board members must be obtained prior to proceeding.*

      "Ascent" means an upward climb or rise, but sounds just like "assent" which means support or agreement.

- Wrong-definition errors use large words that seem like they should mean one thing when really they mean something completely different.
    - Example: *My noisome neighbors are always blasting their music until all-hours of the night.*

      "Noisome" seems like it should have something to do with noise, but really it means foul-smelling.

Pro tip:

If you don't know what a word means, and it's underlined, then there's a very high probability that it is misused. The writing section does not test vocabulary knowledge, so you rarely see obscure words. If you're seeing one, it's probably being tested or used incorrectly.

Practice

Most of the following sentences contain a usage error. Circle the incorrect word or group of words and write in the correct phrase.

1) If the reason for the boy's choosing the one copier over the other was for anything more than the adroitness of the former to produce duplicitous documents, then they were injudicious in their culling process.

2) Mr. Williams claimed that his reason for disliking his neighbors was not their dress, nor the odd hours they kept; he insisted his only concern, despite his known prejudices and predispositions, was their noisome music which sometimes prevented his sleeping.

3) Posthumously, Henry Ford proceeded with his life's work in creating the assembly-line when his son created the interchangeable part after having it obviated that machining individual parts for each car would be inexpedient and imprudent.

4) It was only then that Mrs. Smith realized that she had predisposed the new ticket instead of the used one, thus precluding her from traveling with her compatriots on the train.

5) It was august and usual that the weather had oscillated so sharply from tepid to cold so seamlessly.

6) Contestants' goal is to take an unvalued object from their attics, bring said bauble to market, and have an appraiser proclaim that the gewgaw is esteemed by the intelligentsia, and is worth a high and specific amount: in short, to say it is invaluable.

7) My father is in the habit of trying to fix car problems by dissembling the engine beyond recognition, and then to imbue the scattered parts with some anthropomorphized acrimony toward himself.

8) I proclaimed the painting the most unique I had ever beheld, for it had dynamism, texture, and that *pithy je ne sais quoi* that pervades paintings of its level.

9) The man was quite dead by the time the soldiers found him, and although it was his oft repeated mantra *dolce et decorum est pro patria mori*, the situation was lachrymose and solemn.

10) That the girl is well respected for her work with the poor is no surprise, but the fact that she's infamous also for her singing, caused her friends slightly to be nonplussed at the young woman's meteoric rise to fame.

11) The surplus in the budget was caused by a combination of higher taxes and lower spending, which inferred to the voting public that there had been a fraud perpetrated against the public

12) His lawyer was retained using the privileges granted to indigent defendants, and gave the advise that his client not testify against himself.

13) I do not except his prestidigitation as a reason for your failure to follow the professor's rationale.

14) After all the work the student put in, it was only natural that she be timorous at her graduation: afraid that the situation would be anti-climatic.

15) Our goal in all of these proceedings is to illicit a positive response from the audience after the allusion is complete, not to make them feel duped.

16) Winning basketball games is not only a matter of steadfast determination but of refusing to lay down in front of one's opposition when it comes.

17) The delegate had become inured to the Chicago winter by the time his term was up—so use to the wind and the freezing rain that on rare occasion he would take his constitutional sans coat.

18) Hardly able to believe the consequence, she would not acquiesce to the hypothesis that all animals are suppose to be eaten, and that they are only bred for human enjoyment.

19) I told her I was married, and moved towards the door—not wanting to remove myself from the situation, but concurrently not wanting to betray a trust.

20) Even if what you said corroborated the indigent defendant's story, it would be inconsequential anyways: the evidence was obtained through illegal search and seizure.

21) I am use to my youngest daughter's mendacity, as she is a pathological liar; it is the duplicitousness from my older progeny that I find repugnant.

22) There are alot of reasons to go, and few to stay, she said as she held me with one arm, and her neonatal son in the other.

23) The president spoke largely and claimed that he would effect change among the political discourse in his country—currently one affected—by affecting the almost-dead educational system, and by having a positive effect on privatization of social security.

24) "I will lie down, and then you may lay the lead apron upon me, prior to the X-ray", I said to the doctor yesterday as I lay down on the table and watched as he laid his hand upon the button that was soon to begin the dreaded X-ray machine, one which I had lain down under before, and one which had lain its rays upon me one too many times in the past year.

25) Although some are adverse to chain restaurants, for me they are a reason to wake in the morning: the prognostication of perfectly brewed coffee, the premonition of an egg McMuffin, or the déjà vu of a donut I've had one thousand times before.

26) Sir Edmond Hillary, the first man to make the assent of Everest, and the man after whom the Hillary Step is named, was a mountaineer and a deity among a clique of people that included statesmen, artists, and actors.

27) Mother, the more you ask me if I am already to go, the more I will tarry, for you know my disdain for being rushed.

28) The team member inadvertently lead his opponents to the secret base, not cognizant of his being followed.

29) The instructions on the sunscreen bottle indicated that if one were to lay in the sun for more than twenty minutes, the lotion should be reapplied sparingly.

30) As a boy when I was unable to sleep because of the guilt, my father would admonish me to examine my conscious for blemishes, and though this sentiment was entirely lost on me at the time, I now source it as the seedling of my introspection.

31) It is common for bars to offer their patrons complimentary salty snacks, the theory being that the salty foods induce thirst, and cause the imbibers to further partake.

32) Although the ascent of Mt. Everest is generally considered the more challenging part of the endeavor, it is actually the dissent that inflicts the highest fatality rates on climbers, with a full 25% perishing on their climb down the mountain.

33) Had the prime minister known that the ambassador was in town he would of invited the man to tea, or at least made a pass by his office.

34) On rare occasions, teams will play what is called win-or-go-home match, indicating if one team looses one game, then that team will be ejected from the match and all future competitions, that season.

35) Upper level college courses require, on the whole, perquisites, which require the prospective students to have taken prior courses in the subject or department before the student is permitted to enroll.

36) The starlet's skincare regime was well known throughout Hollywood: biweekly facials, fortnightly peels, and face lifts every third year.

37) Studying thoroughly for the exam which was given once a year, the man was unfettered by seemingly esoteric problems, sense his assiduous preparation had served him well.

38) I would not say her looks are plaintive, at least not to her face, but let us just say, the expression, "Sarah plain and tall" was coined not without the aforementioned in mind.

39) One hears perpetual mention of the perils or pigheadedness of purchasing an extended warrantee, but in all forth righteousness, if the product one is acquiring is error-prone, then perhaps the protection plan is not without merit.

40) As grocery stores are seeking to bolster their diminishing profit margins, they are offering nonstandard services, the manifestations of which are ubiquitously displayed on signs touting, "we will marinade your meat while you wait!" and "ask us to pick out the perfect avocados!"

Answers

1) If the reason for the boy's choosing the one copier over the other was for anything more than the adroitness of the former to produce <u>duplicitous</u> documents, then they were injudicious in their culling process.
   "Duplicitous" means dishonest.

2) Mr. Williams claimed that his reason for disliking his neighbors was not their dress, nor the odd hours they kept; he insisted his only concern, despite his known prejudices and predispositions, was their <u>noisome</u> music which sometimes prevented his sleeping.
   "Noisome" means smelly.

3) Posthumously, Henry Ford proceeded with his life's work in creating the assembly-line when his son created the interchangeable part after having it <u>obviated</u> that machining individual parts for each car would be inexpedient and imprudent.
   "Obviated" means avoided or precluded.

4) It was only then that Mrs. Smith realized that she had <u>predisposed</u> the new ticket instead of the used one, thus precluding her from traveling with her compatriots on the train.
   "Predisposed" means biased.

5) It was <u>august</u> and usual that the weather had oscillated so sharply from tepid to cold so seamlessly.
   "august" (with a lowercase "a") means dignified or noble.

6) Contestants' goal is to take an unvalued object from their attics, bring said bauble to market, and have an appraiser proclaim that the gewgaw is esteemed by the intelligentsia, and is worth a high and specific amount: in short, to say it is <u>invaluable</u>.
   "Invaluable" actually means valuable, but more specifically it means un-priceable, unable to have a value attached to it. The sentence tells us that it's worth a specific amount so we know it's literally by definition valuable.

7) My father is in the habit of trying to fix car problems by <u>dissembling</u> the engine beyond recognition, and then to imbue the scattered parts with some anthropomorphized acrimony toward himself.
   "Dissemble" means hide.

8) I proclaimed the painting the most <u>unique</u> I had ever beheld, for it had dynamism, texture, and that pithy *je ne sais quoi* that pervades paintings of its level.
   There are no levels of unique. "Unique" means completely different. Two things cannot be more or less completely different, they simply are or are not. These are called binary adjectives or adjectives without degrees. Also in this family are "pregnant" and "dead."

9) The man was quite dead by the time the soldiers found him, and although it was his oft repeated mantra *dolce et decorum est pro patria mori*, the situation was lachrymose and solemn.

There are no degrees of death; something either is or is not.

10) That the girl is well respected for her work with the poor is no surprise, but the fact that she's infamous also for her singing, caused her friends slightly to be nonplussed at the young woman's meteoric rise to fame.

"Infamous" means shameful or bad in reputation.

11) The surplus in the budget was caused by a combination of higher taxes and lower spending, which inferred to the voting public that there had been a fraud perpetrated against the public.

Author means "implied." You infer from and imply to.

Example: I inferred from the context that the driver was unhappy even though I did not speak his language. I implied that I was unhappy by frowning.

12) His lawyer was retained using the privileges granted to indigent defendants, and gave the advise that his client not testify against himself.

"Advise" is a verb; the author meant "advice" which is a noun.

13) I do not except his prestidigitation as a reason for your failure to follow the professor's rationale.

"Except" is a preposition, the author means "accept" which is a verb.

14) After all the work the student put in, it was only natural that she be timorous at her graduation: afraid that the situation would be anti-climatic.

"Climatic" has to do with the climate, the author means "climactic" which has to do with a climax.

15) Our goal in all of these proceedings is to illicit a positive response from the audience after the allusion is complete, not to make them feel duped.

Two errors here: "illicit" means illegal; the author means "elicit" meaning to produce.

An "allusion" is a literary reference to another subject; the author means "illusion" which is, in this context, a type of magic trick.

16) Winning basketball games is not only a matter of steadfast determination but of refusing to lay down in front of one's opposition when it comes.

"Lay" needs to be changed to "lie". Loosely you can remember the rule, "things lay, people lie." But the technical explanation is, "lay" is transitive verb (requires an object to follow) unlike "lie" which can stand alone.

Example: Lay the book down. Lie down on the bed.

\

17) The delegate had become inured to the Chicago winter by the time his term was up—so use to the wind and the freezing rain that on rare occasion he would take his constitutional sans coat.

Author means "used to" This is just an attempt to see if you confuse homonyms with their correct forms: "use to" sounds like "used to" but is wrong.

18) Hardly able to believe the consequence, she would not acquiesce to the hypothesis that all animals are suppose to be eaten, and that they are only bred for human enjoyment.

Author means "supposed to". Same explanation as number 17.

19) I told her I was married, and moved towards the door—not wanting to remove myself from the situation, but concurrently not wanting to betray a trust.

There's no error here, British, Australian, and American English all have their preferences for "toward" versus "towards" but neither is incorrect.

20) Even if what you said corroborated the indigent defendant's story, it would be inconsequential anyways: the evidence was obtained through illegal search and seizure.

"Anyways" might soon find its way into the dictionary, but for our purposes it's still considered slang, and should be replaced with "anyway."

21) I am use to my youngest daughter's mendacity, as she is a pathological liar; it is the duplicitousness from my older progeny that I find repugnant.

Change to "used to."

22) There are alot of reasons to go, and few to stay, she said as she held me with one arm, and her neonatal son in the other.

"alot" is not a word; author means, "a lot."

23) The president spoke largely and claimed that he would effect change among the political discourse in his country—currently one affected—by affecting the almost-dead educational system, and by having a positive effect on privatization of social security. NO ERROR

24) "I will lie down, and then you may lay the lead apron upon me, prior to the X-ray", I said to the doctor yesterday as I lay down on the table and watched as he laid his hand upon the button that was soon to begin the dreaded X-ray machine, one which I had lain down under before, and one which had lain its rays upon me one too many times in the past year.

NO ERROR

25) Although some are adverse to chain restaurants, for me they are a reason to wake in the morning: the prognostication of perfectly brewed coffee, the premonition of an egg McMuffin, or the déjà vu of a donut I've had one thousand times before.

"Adverse" means difficult; author means "averse" which means against.

26) Sir Edmond Hillary, the first man to make the assent of Everest, and the man after whom the Hillary Step is named, was a mountaineer and a deity among a clique of people that included statesmen, artists, and actors.
"Assent" means agreement; author means "ascent."

27) Mother, the more you ask me if I am already to go, the more I will tarry, for you know my disdain for being rushed.
Change to "all ready" or "ready."

28) The team member inadvertently lead his opponents to the secret base, not cognizant of his being followed.
"Lead" is the present tense of the verb "to lead;" change to "led" which is past.

29) The instructions on the sunscreen bottle indicated that if one were to lay in the sun for more than twenty minutes, the lotion should be reapplied sparingly.
Change to "lie."

30) As a boy when I was unable to sleep because of the guilt, my father would admonish me to examine my conscious for blemishes, and though this sentiment was entirely lost on me at the time, I now source it as the seedling of my introspection.
"Conscious" is the state of being awake or aware; the author means "conscience" which is one's moral compass.

31) It is common for bars to offer their patrons complementary salty-snacks, the theory being that the salty foods induce thirst, and cause the imbibers to further partake.
"complimentary" (with an "I") means free or flattering. "Complementary" (with an "E") means completing or interdependent.

32) Although the ascent of Mt. Everest is generally considered the more challenging part of the endeavor, it is actually the dissent that inflicts the highest fatality rates on climbers, with a full 25% perishing on their climb down the mountain.
"Dissent" means disagreement; author means "descent."

33) Had the prime minister known that the ambassador was in town he would of invited the man to tea, or at least made a pass by his office.
Change to "would have."

34) On rare occasions, teams will play what is called win-or-go-home match, indicating if one team looses one game, then that team will be ejected from the match and all future competitions, that season.
"Looses"is a verb meaning to unbind. Author means "loses" which is a verb meaning to not win.

35) Upper level college courses require, on the whole, perquisites, which require the prospective students to have taken prior courses in the subject or department before the student is permitted to enroll.

"Perquisites" means perks or advantages; author means "prerequisites" meaning requirements that must be fulfilled prior to doing something.

36) The starlet's skincare regime was well known throughout Hollywood: biweekly facials, fortnightly peels, and face lifts every third year.

A regime is a system of government; author means "regiment."

37) Studying thoroughly for the exam which was given once a year, the man was unfettered by seemingly esoteric problems, sense his assiduous preparation had served him well.

Change to "since."

38) I would not say her looks are plaintive, at least not to her face, but let us just say, the expression, "Sarah plain and tall" was coined not without the aforementioned in mind.

"Plaintive" means pathetic or sad; author means "plain."

39) One hears perpetual mention of the perils or pigheadedness of purchasing an extended warrantee, but in all forth righteousness, if the product one is acquiring is error-prone, then perhaps the protection plan is not without merit.

A "warrantee" is someone to whom a "warranty" is granted. Example: the warrantor granted the warranty to the warrantee. This is similar to saying, "the lessor granted the lease to the lessee."

40) As grocery stores are seeking to bolster their diminishing profit margins, they are offering nonstandard services, the manifestations of which are ubiquitously displayed on signs touting, "we will marinade your meat while you wait!" and "ask us to pick out the perfect avocados!"

Marinade is a noun meaning something you soak meat in; author means "marinate" which is a verb.

CHAPTER 14

Verb Structure

Verb Structure tests your knowledge of three things: tense, mood, and voice.

Tense

By some counts, English has as many as 30 tenses. For the purposes of the SAT, you only really need to focus in on three:

- Simple past: for actions completely concluded in the past.
  - *I ran home.*
- Past perfect: for actions that completely concluded in the past, but which need some emphasis on the order in which they occurred.
  - *I had spoken with her hours before you told me to.*
- Present perfect: for actions that occurred in the past but could still be ongoing.
  - *I have lived in Italy for 3 years (and I still do).*
  - *I have lived in Italy (a long time ago).*

Voice

Keep your verbs in the active voice. I would say it's never appropriate for a verb to be in passive tense on the SAT.

- Active: follows the constructs of Subject + Verb + Object
  - *I cleaned my room.*
  - *We ate the food.*
- Passive: manipulates the traditional syntax into Object + Verb + Subject
  - *My room was cleaned by someone.*
  - *The food was eaten by us.*

Pro Tip:

You can easily identify a passive voice verb because it usually follows this construction:

Thing + Copular ("to be" verb) + Past Tense Verb+ Object

Example:

The dog (object) was (to be) thrown (past) out (preposition) of the house.

The bed (object) is (to be) made (past) by (preposition) the hotel's staff prior to your arrival.

Mood

Do not switch moods within the same sentence.

- Indicative: declaring the certain nature of things.
  - *I am here.*
  - *We will be there tomorrow.*
- Imperative: commands.
  - *Go home.*
  - *Come with us to the party tomorrow.*
- Subjunctive: conjectures about things that are uncertain.
  - *If we went with you, how do you think the hostess would respond?*
    - Notice how the verb goes to a past tense despite talking about something in the future
  - *Be that as it may, we're not leaving you home alone.*
    - Notice how we use a naked infinitive here despite talking about something in the present singular

Pro Tip:

The subjunctive is a vast cavern of confusion, so for our purposes, you only really need be (see that?) familiar with two forms:

If present then future.

If I go, you will come with me.

If subjunctive then conditional.

If I were a cop, I would wear my uniform.

(Notice how we use a past plural verb to refer to a hypothetical singular present event. No need to get wrapped up in the details, all forms of this sentence take the same verb: If I were, If you were, if he/she/it were).

Practice

Many of the verbs in the following sentences are incorrect. Write the proper conjugation above the forms which are incorrect.

1) If we were going to get married next year, then this would have been easier, I think.

2) That was what had to be said to her a few weeks ago, though I regret doing it now.

3) Show me what all the fuss is about, but then you should go to bed.

4) Six days before Valentine's, and two years and eight months after we began dating, the thing was resolving itself to us as we watched on lachrymosely.

5) I don't believe in fate, but if you do, then we are susceptible to disagreements.

6) Only by hanging out in line with the nerds for 3 days were we able to purchase the tickets which had begun to look scarce immediately after we purchased them.

7) Only by hanging out in line with the nerds for 3 days were we able to purchase the tickets which began to look scarce when we were buying them.

8) Only by hanging out in line with the nerds for 3 days were we able to purchase the tickets which were beginning to look scarce long before we had our chance to buy them.

9) I believe by the end of the century, the average American will watch 16000 hours of television by the time he's 5.

10) I believe by the end of the century, the average American will watch 16000 hours of television per month.

11) I believe by the end of the century, the average American will have watched 16000 hours of television more than he will watch in the subsequent centuries.

12) Onlookers looked on as the grammar police had a tense disagreement with the actual police on the topic of tense disagreement, started when the officers posted a sign saying, "If you park in marked spots then your car's towing is ensured."

13) There is no luck involved in my decision to move to a more tropical climate, and in fact I wish I was more persuasive and that I could have convinced you to come with me.

14) My grandfather passed peacefully some years ago, but if he was here, he would wholeheartedly agree with my decision to pursue a degree that would ensure employment post-graduation.

15) Driving home from the concert, where we had been forced to stand for two hours while some opening act tried to get famous on our time, we were just an hour outside of LA when Caroline says that she forgot to close out her tab at the bar.

16) The nanny admonished the parents who were playing with the kids, insisting that it was time the children were in bed.

17) Unlike James who taught in Italy for a couple of years, Jim, you should go teach in Spain until you feel ready to start in the family business.

18) They began construction last year, but unfortunately circumstances arose that would delay the completion, of the grand hotel until next year.

19) The situation was resolved by those who caused it, and as a result we are all the better for it.

20) Since the point in time when the country was dominated by colonial imperialists, it had sought to undo the outside influences of its occupants.

21) The DVD player is dead, so we need to buy a new one.

22) In the time when the politician was active, the country experienced extreme civil unrest which was caused primarily by splinters of factions that have begun to expand in today's world.

23) In the times when the politician has been active, the country had experienced extreme civil unrest which was caused primarily by splinters of factions that have begun to expand in today's world.

24) For the past I-don't-know-how-many years, the old, dilapidated estate served as a kind of meeting place in which young teenagers have been gathering to meet in secret, away from the sidelong glances given by their parents.

25) Before last year, the old, dilapidated estate had served as a kind of meeting place in which young teenagers have been gathering to meet in secret, away from the sidelong glances given by their parents.

26) Last year, the old, dilapidated estate was serving as a kind of meeting place in which young teenagers gathered to meet in secret, away from the sidelong glances given by their parents.

27) He went off to fight in the war, and three years would go by before anyone heard from him.

28) A long time ago, my grandmother would have invited you to stay for tea, share stories with us, etc. but now, please go and leave us to ourselves.

29) Even though the author was previously quite enamored with the media, it was not until June of 1920 that she decided to start being of more use to them by leaking insider stories, and she would come to eventually be dating one of the paparazzi by the end of 1922.

30) She avoided publicity between the 1920s and 1930s, but was thought to have sought out fame in the decades following.

31) She would avoid publicity between the 1920s and 1930s, but was thought to have sought out fame in the decades following.

32) She would have avoided publicity between the 1920s and 1930s, but sought out fame in the decades following.

33) As a witness in a federal trial, I have to admit, if I'm lying then I will pay the ultimate consequence of being convicted of federal perjury.

34) Whether or not I would be here tomorrow would have largely depended on how the results of my performance yesterday would have been interpreted this afternoon, if it is not for the fact that my competitor was disqualified for having been found to have been under the influence of performance-enhancing supplements.

35) To have had the experience you have, and to squander it by retiring at a young age is necessarily spurning everyone who helped you get here.

36) Ask yourself to whom your kids will be listening when you will be greying and criticizing the music that will be produced by your children's children.

37) So you came over to clog my toilet, left when we ran out of food, but insisted the whole time that you have not come merely to take advantage of my hospitality.

38) The psychologist's advice was asinine: she insisted that my past problems were indicative of future ones which she insisted would manifest fourfold if we would not address them in session.

39) The only thing you had ever given me prior to your recovery was a coupon for a buy-one-get-one-free meal which you insist, at the time, would be only valid if I were to take you with me.

40) I read now the same book that I read yesterday.

Answers

1) If we were going to get married next year, then this would have been easier, I think. WOULD BE

   This is an example of one of the two structures of hypotheticals. If subjunctive then conditional: If "we were meant" then "this would."

2) That was what had to be said to her a few weeks ago, and now it is regretted. AND NOW IT IS REGRETTED / THIS IS WHAT I HAD TO SAY

   This is an example of a voice shift error: the voice switches from passive to active within the same sentence.

3) Show me what all the fuss is about, but then you should go to bed. SHOW ME WHAT ALL THE FUSS IS ABOUT AND THEN GO TO BED / YOU SHOULD SHOW ME WHAT ALL THE FUSS IS ABOUT BUT THEN YOU SHOULD GO TO BED

   This is an example of a mood error. The mood shifts from a command form "show me" to declarative " you should."

4) Six days before Valentine's, and two years and eight months after we began dating, the thing was resolving itself to us as we watched on lachrymosely. AS WE WERE WATCHING ON

5) I don't believe in fate, but if you do, then we are susceptible to disagreements. WE WILL BE

6) Only by hanging out in line with the nerds for 3 days were we able to purchase the tickets which had begun to look scarce immediately after we purchased them. BEGAN

7) Only by hanging out in line with the nerds for 3 days were we able to purchase the tickets which began to look scarce when we were buying them. WERE BEGINNING

8) Only by hanging out in line with the nerds for 3 days were we able to purchase the tickets which were beginning to look scarce long before we had our chance to buy them. HAD BEGUN

9) I believe by the end of the century, the average American will watch 16000 hours of television by the time he's 5. WILL HAVE WATCHED

10) I believe by the end of the century, the average American will watch 16000 hours of television per month. WILL BE WATCHING

11) I believe by the end of the century, the average American will have watched 16000 hours of television more than he will watch in the subsequent centuries. WILL WATCH

12) Onlookers looked on as the grammar police had a tense disagreement with the actual police on the topic of tense disagreement, started when the officers posted a sign saying, "If you park in marked spots then your car's towing is ensured" WILL BE ENSURED

13) There is no luck involved in my decision to move to a more tropical climate, and in fact I wish I was more persuasive and that I could have convinced you to come with me. WERE

14) My grandfather passed peacefully some years ago, but if he was here, he would wholeheartedly agree with my decision to pursue a degree that would ensure employment post-graduation. WERE

This is subjunctive and we are assured that it could not be "was" because the person is deceased.

15) Driving home from the concert, where we had been forced to stand for two hours while some opening act tried to get famous on our time, we were just an hour outside of LA when Caroline says that she forgot to close out her tab at the bar. SAID

16) The nanny admonished the parents who were playing with the kids, insisting that it was time the children were in bed. IS

17) Unlike James who taught in Italy for a couple of years, Jim, you should go teach in Spain until you feel ready to start in the family business. JIM, YOU SHOULD GO TEACH IN SPAIN, UNLIKE JAMES WHO TAUGHT IN ITALY FOR A COUPLE OF YEARS, UNTIL YOU FEEL READY….

18) They began construction last year, but unfortunately circumstances arose that would delay the completion, of the grand hotel until next year. DELAYED or WILL DELAY

19) The situation was resolved by those who caused it, and as a result we are all the better for it. VOICE SHIFT: Those who caused the situation resolved it, and as a result.

20) Since the point in time when the country was dominated by colonial imperialists, it had sought to undo the outside influences of its occupants. HAS SOUGHT

21) The DVD player is dead, so we need to buy a new one. PASSIVE/ACTIVE SWITCH: THE DVD PLAYER DIED SO WE NEED TO BUY A NEW ONE.

22) In the time when the politician was active, the country experienced extreme civil unrest which was caused primarily by splinters of factions that have begun to expand in today's world. NO ERROR

23) In the times when the politician has been active, the country had experienced extreme civil unrest which was caused primarily by splinters of factions that have begun to expand in today's world. HAS

24) For the past I-don't-know-how-many years, the old, dilapidated estate served as a kind of meeting place in which young teenagers have been gathering to meet in secret, away from the sidelong glances given by their parents. HAS SERVED

25) Before Last year, the old, dilapidated estate had served as a kind of meeting place in which young teenagers have been gathering to meet in secret, away from the sidelong glances given by their parents. GATHERED/WOULD GATHER

26) Last year, the old, dilapidated estate was serving as a kind of meeting place in which young teenagers gathered to meet in secret, away from the sidelong glances given by their parents. WERE GATHERING

27) He went off to fight in the war, and three years would go by before anyone heard from him. WOULD HEAR

28) A long time ago, my grandmother would have invited you to stay for tea, share stories with us, etc. but now, please go and leave us to ourselves. MOOD SHIFT: BUT NOW WE WILL ASK YOU

29) Even though the author was previously quite enamored with the media, it was not until June of 1920 that she decided to start being of more use to them by leaking insider stories, and she would come to eventually date one of the paparazzi by the end of 1922. DATE

30) She avoided publicity between the 1920s and 1930s, but was thought to have sought out fame in the decades following. NO ERROR

31) She would avoid publicity between the 1920s and 1930s, but was thought to have sought out fame in the decades following. NO ERROR

32) She would have avoided publicity between the 1920s and 1930s, but sought out fame in the decades following. WOULD HAVE SOUGHT

33) As a witness in a federal trial, I have to admit, if I'm lying then I will pay the ultimate consequence of being convicted of federal perjury. I LIE

34) Whether or not I would be here tomorrow would have largely depended on how the results of my performance yesterday would have been interpreted this afternoon, if it is not for the fact that my competitor was disqualified for having been found to have been under the influence of performance-enhancing supplements. WERE IT

35) To have had the experience you have, and to squander it by retiring at a young age is necessarily spurning everyone who helped you get here. TO SPURN.

36) Ask yourself to whom your kids will be listening when you will be greying and criticizing the music that will be produced by your children's children. WILL BE BEING

37) So you came over to clog my toilet, left when we ran out of food, but insisted the whole time that you have not come merely to take advantage of my hospitality. HAD

38) The psychologist's advice was asinine: she insisted that my past problems were indicative of future ones which she insisted would manifest fourfold if we would not address them in session. IF WE DID NOT

39) The only thing you had ever given me prior to your recovery was a coupon for a buy-one-get-one-free meal which you insist, at the time, would be only valid if I were to take you with me. INSISTED

40) I read now the same book that I read yesterday. NO ERROR

CHAPTER 15

Word Pairs

Word pair errors are similar to prepositional errors: the best strategy is practice. Memorize this list, and when you see one of these words come up in a sentence, be sure it is paired with its appropriate partner.

Either X	Or Y
Neither X	Nor Y
Not only X	But Also Y
As X	As Y
Both X	And Y
Between X	And Y
More X	Than Y
Less X	Than Y
So/Such X	That Y
Just as X	So Y
From X	To Y
At once X	And Y
No sooner X	Than Y
Prefer X	To Y
Not so much X	As Y
The reason is X *or*	It is because of Y

Practice

Identify any misused word pairs and correct them.

1) The explosion in the Russian city was atrocious and condemned by all parties, who assumed that the disaster was caused by either a faction of a satellite group whose members included both nationals and foreigners, and conspirators within the capitol.

2) Apple inc, which we now know either for computers or ipods, was once as misguided as the rest of the dot-com startups, thinking it could turn an extra dime by fabricating either clothing, like sweaters or shirts, and by packaging whole PCs in disgusting bright plastic bubbles.

3) Olympic sports come in and out of vogue so rarely that people forget that neither tug-of-war, which was in the Olympics from 1900 to 1920, and wrestling, which was in the games from their inception until 2013, are as prolific as they originally seem.

4) Both dogs, Mia and Sysco being the two most favored of the pack, with their African ancestor the hyena are descendants of the canine species, so named for the location of their canine teeth.

5) As much as he was a treasured friend and a trusted counsel man to his constituents, he was neither as honest nor as transparent in his fiscal dealings with the members of the ministry that he would have the populous believe.

6) As a culture we like to believe that we are the first and the last of a population, when in reality we are not only not as inchoate as we would think but we are not particularly creative—the word "unfriend" first came into publication in the year 1659.

7) Sometimes the thing we need the most is neither as sweet as we remember, either due to a faulty memory or a bittering sentiment, or as saving as we hoped it would be.

8) Neither Morgan Spurlock, famed documentarian who produced FastFood Nation, which was the documentary credited with causing the discontinuation of the SuperSize option, or Michael Moore wanted to touch the issue, considered the third-rail of politics by both left and right-wing groups, both of which said they could not find a justifiable reason to discuss the issue.

9) In Generally Accepted Accounting Principles, the Fair Value of an asset is bounded and must not exceed either the fair value less any selling costs or the greater of sales price less a normal profit less any selling costs, and resale value.

10) Neither the two dogs, either one of which would bite me as soon as look at me, and the two birds, neither the parakeet nor the canary like me at all either, would survive long under my guardianship, for I have a way with animals that almost instantly leads to their demise.

11) Since Colorado legalized the drug, not only have Driving-Under-The-Influence ticket citations increased ten-fold, but prescription sales of medication to treat generalized anxiety disorders have declined sharply.

12) The ship *Not Only* was stranded in the Arctic Circle when a benign research mission not only stranded the *Not Only*, but crippled its main generator, creating a frozen catastrophe miles from aid.

13) Weather forecasts were flowing in through the central distribution center as fast and as accurately that the nimble fingers of the field reporters could type out.

14) The process of arbitration, which can often circumvent the need for expensive and lengthy trials, is as much a benefit to the defendant of the suit, who stands to incur exorbitant legal fees, but to the client of the plaintiff, who himself has no idea what a traditional court battle implies.

15) Bloomberg publishes a list of both the richest people in the world, updated daily and ranked by net worth on that day, with a list of their respective professions and sources of wealth.

16) If the values of America, both hard working determinism concomitant with intellectual aptitude, are compromised for the sake of instant gratification, then the country will surely deteriorate.

17) Both entities which would prosecute, either one of two prosecutorial bodies of the government –the Supreme Court and the House of Representatives—or a specifically appointed Special Prosecutor, will make sure justice is handed down.

18) Between the Middle Ages up to the Renaissance there was an explosion of ideas fostered by better trade routes, globalization, and the need for trade.

19) The phrase by and large is a residual nautical expression used to indicate that a ship was good for sailing both by meaning against the wind, and large meaning with the wind—an expression used widely between 1400 to 1600, when use of the triangle sail first gained prominence.

20) The proverbial finding oneself between a rock—used to reference a difficult situation which is often not circumnavigable—up against a hard place—which would be, in

this case, another unnavigable circumstance, is often used when one's beneficial options are invisible.

21) It was more that the NBA star's visit to the insular dictatorship was perceived as a publicity stunt as opposed to a peacekeeping or goodwill mission that angered the girl whose brother was concurrently being held captive by the country.

22) It's not so much that I detest the old woman, that I just do not like cats, and she seems to have taken it upon herself to be the salvation of that species—which I heretofore didn't perceive as endangered.

23) Current fiscal hawks argue that the prosecution of banks would do less good then harm: in an effort to regulate they would simply stifle.

24) Recent historical endeavors to dispel the myths surrounding glowing Civil War soldiers have actually returned evidence supporting the myth, citing bioluminescent moss which could adhere to soldiers in a way such in they would appear to be glowing.

25) The concept of wind chill is one of those issues which is intuitively simple to grasp, but whose mathematics are such where the actual calculation of the number is near impossible without the assistance of computer models.

26) You are truly your father's son: just as he would dash out for adventure—seeking to tame the Alaskan frontier or to aid the rebels in the Spanish Civil War—you follow in his footsteps in today's world with your computer hacking and your trips to Central America.

27) He swore, upon seeing his land taken from him and his crops burnt before his eyes, just as his forefathers had fled to escape their persecutions, he too would join their ranks and start a new life elsewhere.

28) The Pacific Ocean is such that there is more known about the surface of the moon than there is about the depth that lies below the breadth of the Pacific Ocean which stretches from the Panama Canal clear through the Central African Republic.

29) The classic game *Oregon Trail* was one which pitted its players wits against the trials and tribulations of the wild Oregonian west, on a trail which ran from the middle of the country through regions plagued by dysentery and draught until the promised land of Oregon—provided the player paid to ferry across the river and did not try to be a hero and forge the gap.

30) I cannot stand him, and the reason is because of an event that happened years ago that now only serves to make me sound petty if I try to bring it up.

31) And happening all at once, the summer season changed from sweltering hot and oppressively humid, while the ferry boated the tourists back to their real lives.

32) The two actors were known to be so called frenemies at once hating each other but defending the other fiercely to the relentless paparazzi.

33) Simultaneously, and all at once—redundant as that phrase may be—the author declared that the dog barked when the baby began to cry.

34) Authors whose books eventually become movies are not so much all-devouring egos really, though they are somewhat myopic, as their schedules fill up with appointments and power lunches.

35) Please do not give him as much cake like your brother's portion, as he is diabetic and would probably have to pay a visit to the hospital.

36) Take whatever you want; the reason I bought so many pastries was so that everyone can have as many with their neighbors.

37) Just as you assume that I am arrogant and out-of-touch with the common man simply because I take my coffee with caviar instead of cream and served upon a silver platter carried by ten Olympians, similarly, I think you're equally out of touch with the common man for living in a cave and subsisting on the sap of Vermont maple trees.

38) Let me educate you as to the true nature of coffee: both coffee species are legitimate (Arabica or Robusta) but neither coffee snobs nor laypersons will tell you that the former taste is inferior to the later.

39) The reason you cease to understand art is because you do not understand emotion.

40) Economic crises are rarely caused by a singular event, but rather the reason they are so deleterious is because of this diverse causation: many broken factors coming together to create a perfect storm.

Answers

1) The explosion in the Russian city was atrocious and condemned by all parties, who assumed that the disaster was caused by either a faction of a satellite group whose members included both nationals and foreigners, OR conspirators within the capitol.

2) Apple inc, which we now know either for computers or ipods, was once as misguided as the rest of the dot-com startups, thinking it could turn an extra dime by fabricating either clothing, like sweaters or shirts, OR by packaging whole PCs in disgusting bright plastic bubbles.

3) Olympic sports come in and out of vogue so rarely that people forget that neither tug-of-war, which was in the Olympics from 1900 to 1920, NOR wrestling, which was in the games from their inception until 2013, are as prolific as they originally seem.

4) Both dogs, Mia and Sysco being the two most favored of the pack, AND their African ancestor the hyena are descendants of the canine species, so named for the location of their canine teeth.

5) As much as he was a treasured friend and a trusted counsel man to his constituents, he was neither as honest nor as transparent in his fiscal dealings with the members of the ministry AS he would have the populous believe.

6) As a culture we like to believe that we are the first and the last of a population, when in reality we are not only not as inchoate as we would think BUT ALSO we are not particularly creative—the word "unfriend" first came into publication in the year 1659.

7) Sometimes the thing we need the most is neither as sweet as we remember, either due to a faulty memory or a bittering sentiment, NOR as saving as we hoped it would be.

8) Neither Morgan Spurlock, famed documentarian who produced *FastFood Nation*, which was the documentary credited with causing the discontinuation of the SuperSize option, NOR Michael Moore wanted to touch the issue, considered the third-rail of politics by both left and right-wing groups, both of which said they could not find a justifiable reason to discuss the issue.

9) In Generally Accepted Accounting Principles, the Fair Value of an asset is bounded and must not exceed either the fair value less any selling costs or the greater of sales price less a normal profit less any selling costs, OR resale value.

10) Neither the two dogs, either one of which would bite me as soon as look at me, NOR the two birds, neither the parakeet nor the canary like me at all either, would survive long under my guardianship, for I have a way with animals that almost instantly leads to their demise.

11) Since Colorado legalized the drug, not only have Driving-Under-The-Influence ticket citations increased ten-fold, BUT ALSO prescription sales of medication to treat generalized anxiety disorders have declined sharply.

12) The Ship *Not Only* was stranded in the Arctic Circle when a benign research mission not only stranded the *Not Only*, BUT ALSO crippled its main generator, creating a frozen catastrophe miles from aid.

13) Weather forecasts were flowing in through the central distribution center as fast and as accurately AS the nimble fingers of the field reporters could type out.

14) The process of arbitration, which can often circumvent the need for expensive and lengthy trials, is as much a benefit to the defendant of the suit, who stands to incur exorbitant legal fees, AS to the client of the plaintiff, who himself has no idea what a traditional court battle implies.

15) Bloomberg publishes a list of both the richest people in the world, updated daily and ranked by net worth on that day, AND a list of their respective professions and sources of wealth.

16) If the values of America, both hard working determinism AND intellectual aptitude, are compromised for the sake of instant gratification, then the country will surely deteriorate.

17) Both entities which would prosecute, either one of two prosecutorial bodies of the US government –the Supreme Court and the House of Representatives—AND a specifically appointed Special Prosecutor, will make sure justice is handed down.

18) Between the Middle Ages AND the Renaissance there was an explosion of ideas fostered by better trade routes, globalization, and the need for trade.

19) The phrase *by and large* is a residual nautical expression used to indicate that a ship was good for sailing both *by* meaning against the wind, and *large* meaning with the wind—an expression used widely between 1400 AND 1600, when use of the triangle sail first gained prominence.

20) The proverbial finding oneself between a rock—used to reference a difficult situation which is often not circumnavigable—AND a hard place—which would be, in this case, another unnavigable circumstance, is often used when one's beneficial options are invisible.

21) It was more that the NBA star's visit to the insular dictatorship was perceived as a publicity stunt THAN a peacekeeping or goodwill mission that angered the girl whose brother was concurrently being held captive by the country.

22) It's not so much that I detest the old woman, AS I just do not like cats, and she seems to have taken it upon herself to be the salvation of that species—which I heretofore didn't perceive as endangered.

23) Current fiscal hawks argue that the prosecution of banks would do less good THAN harm: in an effort to regulate they would simply stifle.

24) Recent historical endeavors to dispel the myths surrounding glowing Civil War soldiers have actually returned evidence supporting the myth, citing bioluminescent moss which could adhere to soldiers in a way such THAT they would appear to be glowing.

25) The concept of *wind chill* is one of those issues which is intuitively simple to grasp, but whose mathematics are such THAT the actual calculation of the number is near impossible without the assistance of computer models.

26) You are truly your father's son: just as he would dash out for adventure—seeking to tame the Alaskan frontier or to aid the rebels in the Spanish Civil War—SO TOO you follow in his footsteps in today's world with your computer hacking and your trips to Central America.

27) He swore, upon seeing his land taken from him and his crops burnt before his eyes, just as his forefathers had fled to escape their persecutions, SO TOO would HE join their ranks and start a new life elsewhere.

28) The Pacific Ocean is such that there is more known about the surface of the moon than there is about the depth that lies below the breadth of the Pacific Ocean which stretches from the Panama Canal clear TO the Central African Republic.

29) The classic game *Oregon Trail* was one which pitted its players wits against the trials and tribulations of the wild Oregonian west, on a trail which ran from the middle of the country through regions plagued by dysentery and draught TO the promised land of Oregon—provided the player paid to ferry across the river and did not try to be a hero and forge the gap.

30) I cannot stand him, and the reason is ~~because of~~ an event that happened years ago that now only serves to make me sound petty if I try to bring it up.

31) And happening all at once, the summer season changed from sweltering hot and oppressively humid, AND the ferry boated the tourists back to their real lives.

32) The two actors were known to be so called *frenemies* at once hating each other AND defending the other fiercely to the relentless paparazzi.

33) Simultaneously, and all at once—redundant as that phrase may be—the author declared that the dog barked AND the baby began to cry.

34) Authors whose books eventually become movies are not so much all-devouring egos really, AS they are somewhat myopic, as their schedules fill up with appointments and power lunches.

35) Please do not give him as much cake AS your brother's portion, as he is diabetic and would probably have to pay a visit to the hospital.

36) Take whatever you want; the reason I bought so many pastries was so that everyone can have as many AS their neighbors.

37) Just as you assume that I am arrogant and out-of-touch with the common man simply because I take my coffee with caviar instead of cream and served upon a silver platter carried by ten Olympians, SO TOO, I think you're equally out of touch with the common man for living in a cave and subsisting on the sap of Vermont maple trees.

38) Let me educate you as to the true nature of coffee: both coffee species are legitimate (Arabica AND Robusta) but neither coffee snobs nor laypersons will tell you that the former taste is inferior to the later.

39) The reason you cease to understand art IS THAT you do not understand emotion.

40) Economic crises are rarely caused by a singular event, but rather the reason they are so deleterious IS ~~because of~~ this diverse causation: many broken factors coming together to create a perfect storm.

CHAPTER 16

Test I

Each sentence contains one or no errors. Where sentences contain errors, identify the error and rewrite correctly.

1) You need not be fearful of the consequences, but you need to be cognizant of the gravity of the situation.

2) You cannot, nor should you try to fight the changing tide which so often overcomes us with its insidious encroaching rhythms which placate us one moment and drown us the next.

3) Whether or not I would be here tomorrow would have largely depended on how the results of my performance yesterday would have been interpreted this afternoon, if it is not for the fact that my competitor was disqualified for having been found to have been under the influence of performance-enhancing supplements.

4) When the FBI caught the man who had been hacking into the accounts of celebrities, he commented that it was interesting how all celebrities seemed to date one another, preferring perpetual change to any one person.

5) When completing simple math, it is important to remember the simple premise: one and one are two.

6) We are friends, and since our families have been friends with each other for longer than either of us can remember, I have no reason to predict a terminus.

7) Upper level college courses require, on the whole, perquisites, which require the prospective students to have taken prior courses in the subject or department before the student is permitted to enroll.

8) Unlike those cheesy motivational posters, I would not advise you to simply "Do what you're passionate about" as you must do what is necessary, good, and lucrative, and this may not always tie in to what you'rc passionate about.

9) To have had the experience you have, and to squander it by retiring at a young age is necessarily spurning everyone who helped you get here.

10) They who clean our room should not be relegated to an out-property, but instead let us welcome them into our homes with the warmth they deserve.

11) They tend not to like us as much since the contributions switched their directions.

12) These errands are just eating away the daylight and my productivity, yet they are not necessary the most important things I will do today, despite the hours they require of me.

13) There is a bank located on Birch Street where it crosses Adams, and another which is too far to walk to, but is not far enough to warrant transport via a bus.

14) The two actors were known to be so called frenemies at once hating each other but defending the other fiercely to the relentless paparazzi.

15) The starlet's skincare regime was well known throughout Hollywood: biweekly facials, fortnightly peels, and face lifts every third year.

16) The reasons for the horses' odd behavior is not hard to interpolate: clearly they are underfed and overexposed to the elements.

17) The reasons for the horse's odd behavior is not hard to interpolate: clearly it is underfed and overexposed to the elements.

18) The reason you cease to understand art is because you do not understand emotion.

19) The reason we mark-to-market our accounts so often is to decrease the rampant credit risk of holding unhedged positions.

20) The reason for the horse's odd behavior is not hard to interpolate: clearly it is a combination of being underfed and overexposed to the elements.

21) The pursuer is encouraged to send only one text message, to wait patient until his text message is responded to, and then to respond in kind after an appropriate amount of time has lapsed—as to not seem too eager.

22) The psychologist's advice was asinine: she insisted that my past problems were indicative of future ones which she insisted would manifest fourfold if we would not address them in session.

23) The property manager owned nearly 10,000 square feet of property which was rapidly appreciating on the heels of increasing Net Operating Income numbers which were themselves boosted by increased cap rates.

24) *The Planets*, light years away and celestial by nature, is one of Holst's greatest works, and one that is named after the heavens.

25) The only thing you had ever given me prior to your recovery was a coupon for a buy-one-get-one-free meal which you insist, at the time, would be only valid if I were to take you with me.

26) The male and female administrators of the school were not vindictive in their giving detention to my sister and I, for the punishment that he and she provided to me and her was fair and equitable and commensurate with the crime that he did to her and that she did to him.

27) The lawyer's girlfriend, to whom the lawyer was soon planning on proposing marriage, was going to be in The Hamptons in the Fourth of July, and thus was preparing herself by buying a new swimsuit.

28) The Lakers and the Spurs will never end up playing one another in the post-season, but each is twice the team that they were last season.

29) The depth of the so called Deep Web is deeply unsettling, telling us that the millions of webpages and billions of terabytes of data are not indexed by crawlers and shuttle and show illicit content.

30) The congregation were so bored by the preachers didactic ramblings that, as if by divine intervention, a plan revealed itself unto them which allowed the congregants to cease their attendance without fear of repercussion.

Answers Test I

1) You need not be fearful of the consequences, but you need ~~TO~~ be cognizant of the gravity of the situation. OMIT *The first clause is in the form of the naked infinitive so we need to revise the second clause to the same.*

2) You cannot, nor should you try to fight the changing tide which so often overcomes us with its *insidiously* encroaching rhythms which placate us one moment and drown us the next.
"Insidiously" modifies the gerund "encroaching"

3) Whether or not I would be here tomorrow would have largely depended on how the results of my performance yesterday would have been interpreted this afternoon, WERE IT NOT for the fact that my competitor was disqualified for having been found to have been under the influence of performance-enhancing supplements.

4) When the FBI caught the man who had been hacking into the accounts of celebrities, he commented that it was interesting how all celebrities seemed to date one another, preferring perpetual change to *stability.*

-or-

When the FBI caught the man who had been hacking into the accounts of celebrities, he commented that it was interesting how all celebrities seemed to date one another, preferring perpetually changing partners to any one person. *We don't want to compare perpetual change to a person even if colloquially, we understand what is meant.*

5) When completing simple math, it is important to remember the simple premise: one and one are two. NO ERROR
"One and one" can be thought of as a compound subject, requiring a plural verb. The ear wants the correct version to be "one and one is two" because you want "and" to be a verb meaning, "plus." But it is not.

6) We are friends, and BECAUSE our families have been friends with each other for longer than either of us can remember, I have no reason to predict a terminus.

7) Upper level college courses require, on the whole, perquisites, which require the prospective students to have taken prior courses in the subject or department before the student is permitted to enroll.
"Perquisites" means perks or advantages; author means "prerequisites" meaning requirements that must be fulfilled prior to doing something.

8) Unlike those cheesy motivational posters, I would not advise you to simply "Do what you're passionate about" as you must do what is necessary, good, and lucrative, and this may not always tie in to what you're passionate about. NO ERROR

9) To have had the experience you have, and to squander it by retiring at a young age is necessarily spurning everyone who helped you get here. TO SPURN.

10) They who clean our room should not be relegated to an out-property, but *BE WELCOMED* into our homes with the warmth they deserve.

11) THEY tend not to like us as much since the contributions switched their directions.
"They" is ambiguous and would need to be rewritten to specify.

12) These errands are just eating away the daylight and my productivity, yet they are not *necessarily* the most important things I will do today, despite the hours they require of me.
"Necessarily" is modifying "are"

13) There is a bank located AT Birch Street where it crosses Adams, and another which is too far to walk to, but is not far enough to warrant transport via a bus.

14) The two actors were known to be so called *frenemies* at once hating each other AND defending the other fiercely to the relentless paparazzi.

15) The starlet's skincare regime was well known throughout Hollywood: biweekly facials, fortnightly peels, and face lifts every third year.
A regime is a system of government; author means "regiment."

16) The *reasons* for the horses' odd behavior is not hard to interpolate: clearly they are underfed and overexposed to the elements.

17) The *reasons* for the horse's odd behavior is not hard to interpolate: clearly it is underfed and overexposed to the elements.

18) The reason you cease to understand art IS THAT you do not understand emotion.

19) The reason we so often mark-to-market our accounts is to decrease the rampant credit risk of holding unhedged positions.

20) The reason for the horse's odd behavior is not hard to interpolate: clearly it is a combination of being underfed and overexposed to the elements. NO ERROR

21) The pursuer is encouraged to send only one text message, to wait *patiently* until his text message is responded to, and then to respond in kind after an appropriate amount of time has lapsed—as to not seem too eager.

"Patiently" modifies the verb "wait."

22) The psychologist's advice was asinine: she insisted that my past problems were indicative of future ones which she insisted would manifest fourfold if we would not address them in session. IF WE DID NOT

23) The property manager owned nearly 10,000 square feet of property which was rapidly appreciating on the heels of increasing Net Operating Income numbers which were themselves *BEING BOOSTED BY OR BOOSTED BY* increasing cap rates.

24) One of Holst's greatest works, and one that is named after the heavens, light-years away and celestial by nature, is *The Planets*. NOTE: The Planets is the name of a symphony, and does not refer to the planets themselves.

25) The only thing you had ever given me prior to your recovery was a coupon for a buy-one-get-one-free meal which you insist, at the time, would be only valid if I were to take you with me. INSISTED

26) The male and female administrators of the school were not vindictive in their giving detention to my sister and I, for the punishment that he and she provided to me and her was fair and equitable and commensurate with the crime that he did to her and that she did to him. NO ERROR

27) The lawyer's girlfriend, to whom the lawyer was soon planning on proposing marriage, was going to be in The Hamptons ON the Fourth of July, and thus was preparing herself by buying a new swimsuit.

28) The Lakers and the Spurs will never end up playing one another in the post-season, but each is twice the team that EACH was last season.

29) The depth of the so called *Deep Web* is deeply unsettling, telling us that *CRAWLERS DO NOT INDEX MILLIONS OF WEBPAGES AND BILLIONS OF TERABYTES OF DATA THAT SHUTTLE AND SHOW* illicit content.

We want to avoid switching voices here.

30) The congregation were so bored WITH the preacher's didactic ramblings that, as if by divine intervention, a plan revealed itself unto them which allowed the congregants to cease their attendance without fear of repercussion.

CHAPTER 17

Test II

Each sentence contains one or no errors. Where sentences contain errors, identify the error and rewrite correctly.

1) The circumstances were normal, but, then again, after 20 years of working the Trauma Unit of the ER, there were few things by which the doctor was alarmed.

2) The candidate was dynamic and a gifted public speaker, but even as such, a large percentage of senior citizens are voting against her.

3) The arbitrary arbiter, random and mercurial, errant, albeit not without noble motives, decided to side with the plaintiff in the pollution case.

4) The analyst had a successful half-year review, and with his new salary, he was on target to earn more than last year.

5) Take whatever you want; the reason I bought so many pastries was so that everyone can have as many with their neighbors.

6) Studying thoroughly for the exam which was given once a year, the man was unfettered by seemingly esoteric problems, sense his assiduous preparation had served him well.

7) Students are often made to feel anxious with the large amount of tests they must take prior to graduation.

8) Species of birds are as varied as grains of sand on the beach, but their needs differ little.

9) Some forget that the TV star and her boyfriend formed a band called him and her, and that the crowds of people who pay good money to see he and she play him and her classics are considered some of the most diehard fans in the music industry.

10) So you came over to clog my toilet, left when we ran out of food, but insisted the whole time that you have not come merely to take advantage of my hospitality.

11) Simultaneously, and all at once-redundant as that phrase may be-the author declared that the dog barked when the baby began to cry.

12) Similar to your relationship, an online dating site was where I found my current girlfriend.

13) She would have avoided publicity between the 1920s and 1930s, but sought out fame in the decades following.

14) She would avoid publicity between the 1920s and 1930s, but was thought to have sought out fame in the decades following.

15) She de-friended him on the social networks and said she'd rather not know of the intricacies of status updates, the depths of his likes and dislikes, and the new relationships it relayed back for fear that it would only hurt more acutely.

16) Seth told me that Matt was impressed by his self-sufficiency, implying that military school usually had beneficial results that extended beyond the classroom.

17) Seeming errant methods of calculating the sum of non-converging series can be deceptively simple but also deceptively complex if executed incorrectly.

18) Seek not to operate in a way that brings you happiness, for that is the goal of children, but to conduct yourself in a method that is deliberate angling you toward long term peace and the betterment of those around you.

19) Remember that conflicts are never clean, and that when the French invaded Russia, they ended up retreating in short order only to be plagued by the same years later.

20) Regarding the two rejected players in the corner: you must agree that I and she far prefer the team composed of Payton and Eli to that composed of he and she.

21) Regarding the two rejected players in the corner: you must agree that he and she far prefer the team composed of Payton and Eli to the team that him and her composed.

22) Realizing that he would not be the winner, the racecar driver offered his competitor a handshake in friendship.

23) Ray Bradbury's novels show a preference for suspense and character development over action and instantaneous gratification.

24) Please tell me your brother is not one of those people who, so eagerly, has sprinted headlong into the radical movement.

25) Please do not give him as much cake like your brother's portion, as he is diabetic and would probably have to pay a visit to the hospital.

26) Personified by the anthropomorphic nature of poetry, I was transported by the animals in the works of Ogden Nash, who so adroitly captures their folly and misadventures in his poems.

27) Parliamentary procedure is wrought with inefficiencies, as in the case of disagreements: if the prime minister but not the council members want to pass a resolution, then it would go back to the committee.

28) One hears perpetual mention of the perils or pigheadedness of purchasing an extended warrantee, but in all forth righteousness, if the product one is acquiring is error-prone, then perhaps the protection plan is not without merit.

29) On rare occasions, teams will play what is called win-or-go-home match, indicating if one team looses one game, then that team will be ejected from the match and all future competitions, that season.

30) Obstreperous well-meaning boys are not the norm at our institution, as we are more the type of school that takes demure, knowledge-seeking gentlemen.

Answers: Test II

1) The circumstances were normal, but, then again, after 20 years of working the Trauma Unit of the ER, there were few things AT which the doctor was alarmed.

2) The candidate was dynamic and a gifted public speaker, but even as such, a large percentage of senior citizens are voting against her.

3) The arbitrary arbiter, random and mercurial, *errantly*, albeit not without noble motives, decided to side with the plaintiff in the pollution case.

   This is designed to trick you. You may be used to seeing adjectives in comma-separated lists and might have thought that "errant" was okay. But when you dissect the sentence, you see the first clause "random and mercurial" is a modifier which refers to "arbiter." "Errantly" is modifying "decided" and belongs to the second part of the sentence. If you dropped some of the adjectives, you could read the sentence as, "The arbiter errantly decided to side with the plaintiff."

4) The analyst had a successful half-year review, and with his new salary, he was on target to earn more than *he earned* last year.

5) Take whatever you want; the reason I bought so many pastries was so that everyone can have as many AS their neighbors.

6) Studying thoroughly for the exam which was given once a year, the man was unfettered by seemingly esoteric problems, <u>sense</u> his assiduous preparation had served him well.

   Change to "since."

7) Students are often made to feel anxious BY the large amount of tests they must take prior to graduation.

8) Species of birds are as varied as grains of sand on the beach, but their needs differ little. NO ERROR

9) Some forget that the TV star and her boyfriend formed a band called *him and her,* and that the crowds of people who pay good money to see HIM AND HER play *him and her* classics are considered some of the most diehard fans in the music industry.

   Incidentally, "Him and Her" is the name of a band. But the first instance of the words "Him and Her" are objects that will be seen.

10) So you came over to clog my toilet, left when we ran out of food, but insisted the whole time that you <u>have</u> not come merely to take advantage of my hospitality. HAD

11) Simultaneously, and all at once—redundant as that phrase may be—the author declared that the dog barked AND the baby began to cry.

12) Similar to *where you found* your relationship, an online dating site was where I found my current girlfriend.

-or-

Similar to *you and your relationship*, I found my current girlfriend on an online dating site.

This could also be a misplaced modifier error, but it is a faulty comparison in that "your relationship" is being compared to "an online dating site."

13) She would have avoided publicity between the 1920s and 1930s, but sought out fame in the decades following. WOULD HAVE SOUGHT

14) She would avoid publicity between the 1920s and 1930s, but was thought to have sought out fame in the decades following. NO ERROR

15) She de-friended him on the social networks and said she'd rather not know of the intricacies of status updates, the depths of his likes and dislikes, and the new relationships THEY relayed back for fear that it would only hurt more acutely.

16) Seth told me that Matt was impressed by SETH'S/ MATT'S OWN self-sufficiency, implying that military school usually had beneficial results that extended beyond the classroom.

17) Seemingly errant methods of calculating the sum of non-converging series can be deceptively simple but also deceptively complex if executed incorrectly.

"Seemingly" is modifying "errant"

18) Seek not to operate in a way that brings you happiness, for that is the goal of children, but to conduct yourself in a method that is *deliberately* angling you toward long term peace and the betterment of those around you.

"Deliberately" modifies "angling." It would also be appropriate to put a comma after "deliberate."

19) Remember that conflicts are never clean, and that when the French invaded Russia, *FRANCE/RUSSIA* ended up retreating in short order only to be plagued by the same years later.

"They" is ambiguous and needs to be replaced by one of the countries

20) Regarding the two rejected players in the corner: you must agree that I and she far prefer the team composed of Payton and Eli to that composed of HIM AND HER.

Note the preposition "of" before the pronouns.

21) Regarding the two rejected players in the corner: you must agree that he and she far prefer the team composed of Payton and Eli to the team that HE AND SHE composed.

22) Realizing that HE would not be the winner, the racecar driver offered his competitor a handshake in friendship.

"He" is ambiguous and should be specified.
Now "he and she" are subjects and are "composing."

23) Ray Bradbury's novels show a preference for suspense and character development TO action and instantaneous gratification.

24) Please tell me your brother is not one of those people who, so eagerly, has sprinted headlong into the radical movement. NO ERROR

25) Please do not give him as much cake AS your brother's portion, as he is diabetic and would probably have to pay a visit to the hospital.

26) Personified by the anthropomorphic nature of poetry, *the animals* in the works of Ogden Nash, who so adroitly captures their folly and misadventures in his poems, transported me.

27) Parliamentary procedure is wrought with inefficiencies, as in the case of disagreements: if the prime minister but not the council members WANTS to pass a resolution, then it would go back to the committee.

28) One hears perpetual mention of the perils or pigheadedness of purchasing an extended warrantee, but in all forth righteousness, if the product one is acquiring is error-prone, then perhaps the protection plan is not without merit.

A "warrantee" is someone to whom a "warranty" is granted. Example: the warrantor granted the warranty to the warrantee. This is similar to saying, "the lessor granted the lease to the lessee"

29) On rare occasions, teams will play what is called win-or-go-home match, indicating if one team looses one game, then that team will be ejected from the match and all future competitions, that season.

"Looses" is a verb meaning to unbind. Author means "loses" which is a verb meaning to not win.

30) *Obstreperously* well-meaning boys are not the norm at our institution, as we are more the type of school that takes demure, knowledge-seeking gentlemen.

"Obstreperously" is modifying the adjective phrase "well-meaning"

CHAPTER 17

Test III

Each sentence contains one or no errors. Where sentences contain errors, identify the error and rewrite correctly.

1) Men who gamble frequently are reminded to the duality of their addictions: only losing gamblers have a problem, while winning ones are lucky.

2) Men like we are hardened to such criticisms.

3) Men like us, so we are hardened to such criticisms.

4) Looking at the damage, the doctor estimates that the percentage of the patient's body covered by burns are almost 50%.

5) Let me educate you as to the true nature of coffee: both coffee species are legitimate (Arabica or Robusta) but neither coffee snobs nor laypersons will tell you that the former taste is inferior to the later.

6) Last night it seems we both had the thought that additional subsidies would do more to harm than help the young country.

7) Just as you assume that I am arrogant and out-of-touch with the common man simply because I take my coffee with caviar instead of cream and served upon a silver platter carried by ten Olympians, similarly, I think you're equally out of touch with the common man for living in a cave and subsisting on the sap of Vermont maple trees.

8) Jeff told Jim that he was a better attorney when he was attending regular meetings, and that the program has a lower recidivism rate than other forms of recovery.

9) It's a fairly cushy gig: stay up and watch the dogs pace if you need something to keep you alert during the long nights.

10) It might be uncouth to like a corporately-produced product this much, but I love the taste of iced coffee that is made just for me.

11) It is common for bars to offer their patrons complimentary salty snacks, the theory being that the salty foods induce thirst, and cause the imbibers to further partake.

12) Insufficient funded classes are one of the main reasons that schools in certain countries are at such a disadvantage relative to others.

13) In the tired and worn-out post-test phase of the six-hour exam, the candidates agreed that this year was far more challenging than the test of last year.

14) In forgotten depths of darkness lie the places angels deign to fly, and in those depths where loss is found, a deafening din is said to sound like retreating fervor on love's last ground, and those who fight won't last the night, but still insist their cause is right, honorable, and worth the plight.

15) In areas of strength, as in weakness, it is important to have perspective and realize that you are not the worst, nor the best, just another one trying to excel, fighting your own battles.

16) I'm younger than he, so it should be me who is the first to roll the die.

17) I'm sorry, as I missed the first part of the conversation and the finale of the race; you are faster than who?

18) If you allow that Picasso was a precursor of Rothko then you must simultaneously allow that Monet and Cezanne were precursors of Serat.

19) I would not say her looks are plaintive, at least not to her face, but let us just say, the expression, "Sarah plain and tall" was coined not without the aforementioned in mind.

20) I would give the appropriate approbation to he who is found in possession of a working knowledge of the different pronoun cases: nominative, objective, possessive.

21) I was singularly unimpressed by the nominees this year, and found no one to be better than any of the nominees.

22) I was fortified by the fruits of the land, made hard by the slings of my opponents, calloused by their comments, and so can you.

23) I read now the same book that I read yesterday.

24) I only posit that Einstein, being the one who brought us the two pillars of physics, is one of the greatest mathematicians who has ever lived.

25) I misunderstood the questions' purposes which were to illustrate the intelligence of the asker, not condemn the stupidity of the answerer.

26) I know which book you are talking about, but this is not one of those Drug Store Novels, so many of which do not warrant the death of a tree for their printing, which deals with the subject of long lost love.

27) I give you the countries of Zimbabwe and Malawi as an examples of places where the average life expectancy is decreasing.

28) I encourage everyone to enjoy the ride, as we cannot be sure if any moment will be better than the last or worse than the prior.

29) How are we supposed to find our way out of the labyrinth when none of us know our cardinal directions?

____

____

____

____

30) His superiors granted him the promotion he requested, recognizing in him a strong ability for problem solving and client interactions.

____

____

____

____

Answers Test III

1) Men who frequently gamble are/who gamble are frequently reminded of the duality of their addictions: only losing gamblers have a problem, while winning ones are lucky.

2) Men like US are hardened to such criticisms.

   "Like" is a preposition here, so the proper pronoun to use is an object pronoun.

3) Men like US, so we are hardened to such criticisms. No Error

4) Looking at the damage, the doctor estimates that the percentage of the patient's body covered by burns IS almost 50%.

5) Let me educate you as to the true nature of coffee: both coffee species are legitimate (Arabica AND Robusta) but neither coffee snobs nor laypersons will tell you that the former taste is inferior to the later.

6) Last night it seems we both had the thought that additional subsidies would do more to harm than help the young country. NO ERROR

7) Just as you assume that I am arrogant and out-of-touch with the common man simply because I take my coffee with caviar instead of cream and served upon a silver platter carried by ten Olympians, SO TOO, I think you're equally out of touch with the common man for living in a cave and subsisting on the sap of Vermont maple trees.

8) Jeff told Jim that JIM/JEFF was a better attorney when he was attending regular meetings, and that the program has a lower recidivism rate than other forms of recovery. *"He" is ambiguous.*

9) It's a fairly cushy gig: stay up and watch the dogs; pace if you need something to keep you alert during the long nights.

   Place a semicolon after "dogs."

10) It might be uncouth to like a corporately-produced product this much, but I love the taste of Starbucks iced coffee *THAT BARISTAS MAKE FOR ME.*

   There's a voice shift in "love"(active) to "is made"(passive). Change them to match.

11) It is common for bars to offer their patrons complementary salty snacks, the theory being that the salty foods induce thirst, and cause the imbibers to further partake.

   "compmlimentary" (with an "I") means free or flattering. "Complementary" (with an "E") means completing or interdependent.

12) *Insufficiently* funded classes are one of the main reasons that schools in certain countries are at such a disadvantage relative to others.

"Insufficiently" modifies the adjective "funded"

13) In the tired and worn-out post-test phase of the six-hour exam, the candidates agreed that this year's test was far more challenging than *the test of* last year.

14) In forgotten depths of darkness lie the places angels deign to fly, and in those depths where loss is found, a deafening din is said to sound like retreating fervor on love's last ground, and those who fight won't last the night, but still insist their cause is right, honorable, and *WORTHY*.

There are any number of ways to change this. It doesn't matter what you choose, just realize that "worth the plight" is incongruous with "right, honorable"

15) In areas of strength, as in *areas of* weakness, it is important to have perspective and realize that you are not the worst, nor the best, just another one trying to excel, fighting your own battles.

16) I'm younger than he, so it should be I who is the first to roll the die.

If this sounds off, just remember the copular rule "be" goes with subject pronouns.

17) I'm sorry, as I missed the first part of the conversation and the finale of the race; you arc faster than who? NO ERROR

18) If you allow that Picasso was a precursor of Rothko then you must simultaneously allow that Monet and Cezanne were *precursors* of Serat.

19) I would not say her looks are plaintive, at least not to her face, but let us just say, the expression, "Sarah plain and tall" was coined not without the aforementioned in mind.

"Plaintive" means pathetic or sad; author means "plain"

20) I would give the appropriate approbation to HIM who is found in possession of a working knowledge of the different pronoun cases: nominative, objective, possessive.

Use the preposition rule "to" right before the pronoun demands an object pronoun.

21) I was singularly unimpressed by the nominees this year, and found no one to be better than any of the *other* nominees.

22) I was fortified by the fruits of the land, made hard by the slings of my opponents, calloused by their comments, and so can you. NO ERROR

There is an implied, "so can you be made so" so there is no error.

23) I read now the same book that I read yesterday. NO ERROR

24) I only posit that Einstein, being the one who brought us the two pillars of physics, is one of the greatest mathematicians who has ever lived. NO ERROR

25) I misunderstood the questions' *purposes* which were to illustrate the intelligence of the asker, not condemn the stupidity of the answerer.

26) I know which book you are talking about, but this is not one of those Drug Store Novels, so many of which do not warrant the death of a tree for their printing, which deals with the subject of long-lost love. NO ERROR

27) I give you the countries of Zimbabwe and Malawi as ~~an~~ *examples* of places where the average life expectancy is decreasing.

28) I encourage everyone to enjoy the ride, as we cannot be sure if any moment will be better than the last or worse than the prior. NO ERROR

29) How are we supposed to find our way out of the labyrinth when none of us know our cardinal directions? NO ERROR

30) His superiors granted him the promotion he requested, recognizing in him ~~a~~ strong *abilities* for problem solving and client interactions.

CHAPTER 18

Test IV

Circle the incorrect portion of each sentence.

1) He thinks about her all the time, but insists that he made the right choice, and that in the end he will be responsible for having saved their lives, though he never expects her to see that.

2) He showed me the sentence, "let's eat grandma" and, "let's eat, grandma" and dared me to again insist, as I had previously, those commas that are used frequently are misused.

3) Having had the faith that he had had, the minister was undaunted by the fact that, halved, his church attendance was reduced.

4) Had the prime minister known that the ambassador was in town he would of invited the man to tea, or at least made a pass by his office.

5) Effectively ending his racing career, the man was struck by the strangeness of the situation in watching a horse who had spent his whole life racing succumb to a condition as nonthreatening as gout, caused by the jockey giving him too much rich food.

6) Economic crises are rarely caused by a singular event, but rather the reason they are so deleterious is because of this diverse causation: many broken factors coming together to create a perfect storm.

7) Earning one's fortune is far preferable to the lottery victory, as the former will provide you with a linear sense of success, while the latter will be like an explosion in your life.

8) Don't be surprised if, when asked about their financial statuses, wages, taxes, charitable contributions, many people's first reaction is silence.

9) Divers know that an overly-quick return to the surface can result in The Bends, an illness that for most is extremely detrimental for the health.

10) Cinematic showy movies are the stuff of awards shows and art house premiers, but I prefer a good cartoon any day.

11) Christine's bull was disinclined to charge the red flags waved in front of him, and far preferred to sit under a tree and smell the flowers she would find.

12) Charles, Baxter, and Sophie are Springer Spaniels with traditional haircuts, but his tail is clipped while the other two have full tails.

13) Buffalo buffalo Buffalo buffalo buffalos buffalo Buffalo buffalo. (Hint: "buffalo" is a verb meaning, to intimidate)

14) Becoming a grandmaster, the openings of chess, the gambits, and the point-value of pieces must be mastered.

15) Be it us who are called to fight the fire or be it the fire brigade of the other city, the fire will be fought by they who are called.

16) Authors whose books eventually become movies are not so much all-devouring egos really, though they are somewhat myopic, as their schedules fill up with appointments and power lunches.

17) At times, one has to wonder why people chose to inhabit Australia: started as a penal colony of the British, it is now home to a species of jellyfish whose venom is the only thing more poisonous than a bite by one of their legendary spiders.

18) Ask yourself to whom your kids will be listening when you will be greying and criticizing the music that will be produced by your children's children.

19) As grocery stores are seeking to bolster their diminishing profit margins, they are offering nonstandard services, the manifestations of which are ubiquitously displayed on signs touting, "we will marinade your meat while you wait!" and "ask us to pick out the perfect avocados!"

20) As a witness in a federal trial, I have to admit, if I'm lying then I will pay the ultimate consequence of being convicted of federal perjury.

21) Although the ascent of Mt. Everest is generally considered the more challenging part of the endeavor, it is actually the dissent that inflicts the highest fatality rates on climbers, with a full 25% perishing on their climb down the mountain.

22) All staff meetings are important, but for this one, the principal made a heartfelt plea that no teachers be absent at the congregation, for she had a special announcement.

23) After the analyst took his Series 7 exam, a 7 hour test, he was tired, was thirsty, and fearful that his score was not high enough.

24) After the analyst took his Series 7 exam, a 7 hour test, he was tired, thirsty, and was fearful that his score was not high enough.

25) After the analyst took his Series 7 exam, a 7 hour test, he was tired and thirsty, and was fearful that his score was not high enough.

26) A strict city ordinance, not to mention the common sense employed by the populous, dictates to the masses that they are prohibited to ride bicycles on highways.

27) A financial analyst, quantitatively-minded and good with computers, adroit, and with a strong fundamental knowledge of financial processes and valuations, is able to determine the value of equities and assign them relative ratings.

28) And happening all at once, the summer season changed from sweltering hot and oppressively humid, while the ferry boated the tourists back to their real lives.

29) The need of the community is not the same as the needs of the members who want for access to healthcare and clean water.

30) A non-negligible percentage of actors, regardless of individual country of origin, partake of the Japanese delicacy, sashimi.

Answers Test IV

1) He thinks about her all the time, but insists that he made the right choice, and that in the end he will be responsible for having saved their lives, though he never expects her to see that. NO ERROR

2) He showed me the sentence, "let's eat grandma" and, "let's eat, grandma" and dared me to again to insist, as I had previously, those commas that are frequently used are misused.

3) Having had the faith that he had had, the minister was undaunted by the fact that, halved, his *church's attendance was reduced.*

4) Had the prime minister known that the ambassador was in town he <u>would of</u> invited the man to tea, or at least made a pass by his office.

   Change to "would have."

5) Effectively ending the horse's career, the man was struck by the strangeness of the situation in watching a horse who had spent his whole life racing succumb to a condition as non-threatening as gout, caused by the jockey giving him too much rich food.

6) Economic crises are rarely caused by a singular event, but rather the reason they are so deleterious IS ~~because of~~ this diverse causation: many broken factors coming together to create a perfect storm.

7) Earning one's fortune is far preferable to *winning the lottery*, as the former will provide you with a linear sense of success, while the latter will be like an explosion in your life.

   This is almost a parallelism error, but we're comparing "earning" to "the lottery victory" so it would be better to compare "earning" to "winning."

8) Don't be surprised if, when asked about their financial status—wages, taxes, charitable contributions—many people react with silence at first.

9) Divers know that an overly-quick return to the surface can result in The Bends, an illness that for most is extremely detrimental TO the health.

10) *Cinematically* showy movies are the stuff of awards shows and art house premiers, but I prefer a good cartoon any day.

   "Cinematically" is modifying the adverb "showy."

11) Christine's bull was disinclined to charge the red flags waved in front of him, and far preferred to sit under a tree and smell the flowers HE would find.

12) Charles, Baxter, and Sophie are Springer Spaniels with traditional haircuts, but BAXTER'S/CHARLE'S tail is clipped while the other two have full tails.

"His" is ambiguous.

13) Buffalo buffalo Buffalo buffalo BUFFALO buffalo Buffalo buffalo. (Hint: buffalo is a verb meaning, to intimidate)

This sentence is a classic. It hinges on the fact that you don't need the words "that" to make a complete sentence. Here's the explanation:

Buffalo buffalo (the animal from the city of Buffalo) (THAT OTHER) Buffalo buffalo (animals from the city of Buffalo) buffalo (meaning bother)(THEMSELVES) buffalo (meaning bother) Buffalo buffalo (animals from the city of Buffalo)

It's like saying "New York people that New York people bother, they themselves, bother New York people."

At any rate, the subject is plural so it needs a plural verb.

14) To become a grand master, the openings of chess, the gambits, and the point-value of pieces must be mastered.

15) Be it us who are called to fight the fire or be it the fire brigade of the other city, the fire will be fought by they who are called.

16) Authors whose books eventually become movies are not so much all-devouring egos really, though they are somewhat myopic, as their schedules fill up with appointments and power lunches.

17) At times, one has to wonder why people chose to inhabit Australia: started as a penal colony of the British, it is now home to a species of jellyfish whose venom is the only thing more poisonous than *the venom from* a bite by one of their legendary spiders.

18) Ask yourself to whom your kids will be listening when you will be greying and criticizing the music that will be produced by your children's children. WILL BE BEING

19) As grocery stores are seeking to bolster their diminishing profit margins, they are offering nonstandard services, the manifestations of which are ubiquitously displayed on signs touting, "we will marinade your meat while you wait!" and "ask us to pick out the perfect avocados!"

Marinade is a noun meaning something you soak meat in; author means "marinate" which is a verb.

20) As a witness in a federal trial, I have to admit, if I'm lying then I will pay the ultimate consequence of being convicted of federal perjury. I LIE

21) Although the ascent of Mt. Everest is generally considered the more challenging part of the endeavor, it is actually the <u>dissent</u> that inflicts the highest fatality rates on climbers, with a full 25% perishing on their climb down the mountain.

"Dissent" means disagreement; author means "descent."

22) All staff meetings are important, but for this one, the principal made a heartfelt plea that no teachers be absent FROM the congregation, for she had a special announcement.

23) After the analyst took his Series 7 exam—a 7 hour test—he was tired, was thirsty, and *WAS* fearful that his score was not high enough.

24) After the analyst took his Series 7 exam—a 7 hour test—he was tired, *WAS* thirsty, and was fearful that his score was not high enough.

25) After the analyst took his Series 7 exam—a 7 hour test—he was tired and thirsty, and was fearful that his score was not high enough. NO ERROR

But it could also be revised, "and fearful that."

26) A strict city ordinance, not to mention the common sense employed by the populous, dictates to the masses that they are prohibited to ride bicycles on highways. NO ERROR

27) A financial analyst, quantitatively-minded and good with computers, adroit, and with a strong fundamental knowledge of financial processes and valuations, is able to determine the value of equities and assign them relative ratings.

Correct as is. Also this would be grammatically correct to interchange "adroit" with "adroitly."

28) And happening all at once, the summer season changed from sweltering hot and oppressively humid, AND the ferry boated the tourists back to their real lives.

29) The need of the community is not the same as the *needs* of the members who want for access to healthcare and clean water.

30) A non-negligible percentage of actors, regardless of individual country of origin, *partakes* of the Japanese delicacy, sashimi.

86336495R00129

Made in the USA
San Bernardino, CA
28 August 2018